A YIN FOR CHANGE

Books by Sonny Brewer

REMBRANdT the Rocker

Red Bluff Review
(an anthology, as Editor)

For Wade—
Please let me know
what you think about
my friend William Gay.

A YIN FOR CHANGE

Awakening imagination
for more life in your living

or   *all my best*
to you!

"If you don't like the gumbo,
fool around with the recipe
until it tastes better."

Sonny Brewer

June 2002

Over the Transom Publishing Company

For information about the book
or the author as a guest speaker, contact:
Over the Transom Publishing Company
P.O. Box 639, Fairhope, Alabama 36533
1-334-990-7980

Second Printing

ISBN 0-9643727-1-1

*This book is dedicated to
Richard Baronian Shackelford*

Acknowledgments

I want to thank everyone—you are legion—who tossed in two cents' worth to *A Yin for Change*. Your comments and suggestions have been worth far more, in some cases even twice that.

I am especially grateful to Diana, my wife, and to Kendra Utsey, Kyle Jennings, Dr. Jack Davis, Reverend Adrian Cook, and Suzanne Barnhill, and to my children, Emily, John Luke, and Dylan, who show me every day the workings of Yin Mind.

Contents

One

AND NOW, BY POPULAR DEMAND, YET ANOTHER BOOK

For a few years now I've been a lecturer with a local university's elderhostel program. Elderhostel is offered internationally by colleges and universities to people of at least retirement age. Typically, for one price, elderhostelers get room and board and classes exploring one or several topics: you might go to Madrid for a couple of weeks to learn Spanish, to New York for five days to learn "How Broadway Plays Are Produced," or to New Orleans to take a smorgasbord of classes in everything from Creole history and genealogy to "Cooking with Hot Sauce" and nightly tours of the town.

Since I've been a journalist, editor, and publisher and have written a children's book for kids over sixty called *REMBRANdT the Rocker,* I typically find myself included on the elderhostel agenda as a speaker in the writing workshops. Those sessions are most fun when I talk about creativity, and it occurred to me that elderhostelers with not a whit's interest in writing might also enjoy and benefit from welcoming a little more creativity into their lives.

So I hornswoggled the director into including me in the non-writing programs for a single hour-and-forty-five-minute talk called "Using Your Whole Brain." That's the title listed in the elderhostel class directory. Listed that way it probably snags some students who think I've found a secret way to use the ninety percent of our brains they say we don't use.

But what I talk about is Yin Mind, more popularly known as Right Brain Thinking— highly creative, nonverbal, and intuitive intelligence that some say resides in the right hemisphere of our brains.

Someone writing in the *New Scientist* declared that experimental evidence is now mounting that the hitherto neglected cerebellum is the true seat of the emotional-unconscious mind and not the right hemisphere of the brain. But I have not signed on to the location controversy. Intuitive intellect may, for all I care, reside in your left ankle. What I *know* is that we view our world in a dualistic manner. The ancient Chinese divided our perception of things into two lists: yin and yang.

Here's a yang perception: A khaki-clad young woman in her photographer's vest goes outside, adjusts her Ray-Bans and looks up at the sky and declares cirrocumulus at an altitude of 12,000 feet, moving in a westerly direction at about seven to ten knots.

And a yin perception of the same: A white-haired fellow wearing Birkenstock sandals, sporting a dangly gold earring, who gazes into what Emerson called "the daily bread of the eye" and dreamily describes the hippopotamus he sees skidding down a long wispy sliding board into a pool of water.

I think Einstein was right about imagination being more important than knowledge. Not that knowledge is not important; on the contrary, imagination leads to more knowledge. And since I believe our faculties for imagination are often neglected, I like to sell imagination and intuition and creativity in my elderhostel talks. And instead of Right Brain Thinking I call it Yin Mind.

I have frequently been asked by the elderhostelers to "write it down." When I walk into one of those forty-acre bookstores, complete with a coffee cafe in the corner, I wonder why another book . It's all been said. But then God didn't stop with one pine tree. So I'll just go ahead and add my seedling to the forest.

And a thin book it will be—like a used car salesman's book of ethics. (I wrote an outline for that book when I made my living selling cars.) My attention span is too short for a long work. I've already ordered my gravestone and the epithet reads: "If this is anything like his life, he won't be here long." So I promise not to keep you overlong.

And while we are gathered together, I'll invite you (as I do each of my elderhostelers) to doubt all that I say. After all, I sold used cars. And I admit that I'd never let the truth stand in the way of a good story. So dump the lawn trimmings from your wheelbarrow, hightail it to the bookstore or public library, and load it with books. I like to buy books so I can underline for quick reference. But whether you buy or borrow the books, go ahead, make my day: catch me in a lie, catch me in a misquote. If we read enough books, maybe we can identify the plagiarists in our midst. Don't look for a bibliography at the end of this book (or an index for that matter). My suggested reading list is on almost every page.

Friends tell me I quote others a lot and ask me, "But how do *you* feel, Sonny, about the matter?" The same, of course, as the fellow I'm quoting. Let's just say that quoting someone else seems to add weight to my opinion by invoking a greater, better-known authority. I mean, if Jesus and I agree on something, if he is with me, who could be against me? At base, though, is the awareness that authority gets its authority from those it governs. If Emerson is an authority, you and I *allow* him to be.

On the other hand, it has occurred to me that I don't really know what Jesus *actually* said. Or what Oscar Wilde said. Or William James. Or Shakespeare. (Or which anecdote belongs to whom.) Everybody's running around stealing from everyone else, and it's been going on for so long that I wonder if anyone has ever said anything original.

I've read that Goethe said: "Everything has been thought of before. The problem is to think of it again." And, I might add, get away with taking credit for thinking of it again. An artist I know got caught "slightly copying" artwork from a 1920s Coca-Cola poster onto what proved to be for her a best-selling lithograph. Didn't it dawn on her that there would be no such thing as an "obscure" Coca-Cola item from which to draw inspiration?

I read in Carleen Franklin's little *Treasure Book of Affirmations for Personal Fulfillment* that William James said: "The greatest revelation of our generation is the discovery that human beings, by changing the inner attitude of their minds, can change the outer aspects of their lives." There in one pithy little aphorism is what I will ramble through all these pages to say. The heart and soul of Yin Mind is a willingness to change your mind.

But who am I siding with when I use the aforementioned quote? Because on page 411 of *Alternative Medicine* I read that Albert Schweitzer said: "The greatest discovery of any generation is that human beings can alter their lives by altering the attitude of their minds." Will the real soothsayer please stand up?

Some stories I've read about Jesus I find myself reading again in stories about Buddha. Perhaps I should just leave off ascribing a quote to Emerson or Thoreau, doctor up a little what I've read each said, and say something like: "I think country lads who dance to a different fiddler are worth more than a thousand city dolls prancing in lockstep to the latest popular ditty." I remember a politician who got into trouble for stealing the thoughts and words of "weightier authorities." When cries of plagiarism rang out, I was incredulous.

I heard the other day on public radio that emerging capitalism is having trouble in China. Your standard copyright rip-offs are occurring there with alarming frequency. The commentator said there is an obvious criminal element at work, but that some thought must also be given to oriental philosophies that say the product of one mind belongs to all minds. Like the old Indian chief who wonders about the Big Bellies in Washington offering him title to land. How, he wonders, can you take title to your mother? What belongs to all cannot be sold or titled.

So read critically. In Lin Yutang's book, *The Importance of Living,* he recommends that we not strive so hard, for instance, to find all the typos in a manuscript set for publication. Why deny the reader that exquisite and perverse pleasure she gets from finding the mistake? Open some books and find out for yourself who said what. Then you'd better double-check for accuracy. And be prepared to admit, later, that you've been wrong.

But don't tell me because I don't care who grows the celery or the rice, or who catches the shrimp or tongs the oysters that go into my pot of gumbo. When I am finished cooking and stirring it up, it'll be *my* pot of gumbo no matter whose ingredients I've tossed in. That's what I'm serving you here: my own world view and theology.

And, speaking of theology, if I sometimes sound preachy, just remember, it is *me* I am trying to reach. My great-uncle told me that in forty years as a Congregational minister, every time he took the pulpit it was himself he was addressing. "I knew that if anybody in the building needed a reminder that using the truth to convey a falsehood is still a lie, it was me." He told me this clever little sermon came up after he'd answered his wife's query: "John, did you do what I asked you to do for me?" The question, he said, was general enough that he could answer yes, for he had, indeed, at one time or another, done what she asked. He knew, however, he had not yet done the specific thing she requested of him.

Montaigne wrote a little note to the reader in the last volume of his essays that said, in part: "Thus, reader, I myself am the matter of my book: there's no reason thou shouldst employ thy

17

leisure about so frivolous and vain a subject.
Therefore, farewell." That was penned on 12
June 1580, and we're still reading. So, in advance,
farewell, therefore, if you choose not to share this
pot of gumbo with me.

Hey! Wait, did you hear the one about green
eggs and ham? You know, Dr. Seuss's story about
Sam-I-Am trying to get the fellow to try a bite of
green eggs and ham. The fellow spent the entire
book telling Sam-I-Am he did not like green eggs
and ham. But when he finally tried them he loved
them. Keep reading, then, even if now this all
sounds yucky.

Two

BUT I JUST BOUGHT THESE GLOVES

Imagine this: The year is 1979. You're invited to board a bus and come along on an all-expense-paid week-long trip back in time twenty years. You and all the other adventurers will be men seventy-five or older. When the Greyhound reaches its destination you will find yourselves at a country resort that has the look of 1959. Maybe you'll spot a '55 T-bird and a '57 Chevy parked along the curb; the newspaper and radio stories tell of Ike's latest golf game—you get the picture.

You're asked to bring along a photo of yourself circa 1959. The snapshot will be used on a name tag that you'll wear all week long.

While at the resort, if you discuss current events, nothing past 1959, please. When Frankie

Lane is crooning on the radio, don't even think of mentioning the invasion of British rock'n'roll and the "twist" or the "mashed potatoes."

Even though you're retired, talk about your careers as though you're on vacation and will be reporting back to the office when this little vacation is over

Maybe you've caught on to the catch. (You knew there'd be a catch!) Only the retreat setting is 1959. No *Star Trek* time warping has occurred. You are still smack dab in the middle of 1979. You're going to have to use "psychological intervention" to coax your mind back through the years and only pretend to be twenty years younger. Our retreat setting and the rules of the game, however, are designed to make it easier for you to do that.

Besides being a fun thing to do, what else would such an experience yield for its participants? Just ask Ellen Langer, a Harvard psychology professor. Several people accepted her invitation in 1979 to do just what we've described. Langer subsequently published the results this playacting had on the participants.

Certain "biological markers" were recorded for each man who went on the mind expedition to 1959, including everything from IQ to finger length.

Deepak Chopra talked about Ellen's study in his book *Ageless Body, Timeless Mind.* He writes of all kinds of neat things that happened to these old men who pretended to rip a couple of decades off the calendar. They got stronger and smarter, remembered better, stood up straighter, moved their body parts about with greater ease, saw things more clearly, even began to look younger. And—this is wild—they got longer fingers in the deal!

See, as you age, your fingers get shorter. But these men got on the bus home with longer fingers. Oscar Wilde said that once you stretch your mind with a new idea, it never returns to its original size. So even though our time travelers might have regressed back to the same glove size in a matter of weeks, their minds had been stretched with a new idea: the striking realization that there is unlimited potential for changing the outer aspects of their lives by merely changing the inner attitude of their minds. Even if these guys were closing in on the century mark.

It is a fact that your little three-pound personal computer is losing weight as you get older, but maybe they aren't such precious ounces after all. Your mind isn't limited by your brain *size.* Who needs a fat brain? How big were the first IBM computers? Today you can lose your computer between credit cards in your wallet.

And here's some metaphysical conjecture for you: I don't even believe the mind lives among those gray wrinkles. It merely shows up for work there and at night, in your dreams, roams around like a drunken monkey all over the universe.

This is *not* conjecture: your mind is proven to have the capacity to install new dendrites to compensate for the brain's loss of mass and weight with aging. Dendrites (from the Greek word for tree) are little filaments in the brain's wiring system along which information travels. So even when you are old you can grow more branches, you might say, for your squirrel-like thoughts to leap around upon. Only, however, if you use your mind do you get new dendrites. "Use it or lose it!" never meant more.

Take heart, then: no matter what your age, you are absolutely free to change your attitude. And thereby your actual physiological circumstances, without even leaving the comfort of your own home. Life is not a box of chocolates where, as Forrest Gump's momma taught him, "You never know what you're gonna get." You might indeed get something unexpected, but life is still cooking, like a big pot of gumbo. And if you don't like the way the gumbo tastes, fool around with the recipe until it tastes better!

The problem for most of us, anyway, is that we've been handed recipes for living we believe are chiseled onto something akin to Moses' tablets. We behave like hirelings in the kitchen who fear that to make changes to society's joint-stock recipes will get us a meat cleaver to the neck.

Au contraire. (Translation: *bull pucky!*)

That kind of *girl-your-mother-is-watching-you* thinking is merely yang-thinking, or, to many, left hemisphere dominance.

Processing too much Yang Mind causes the wrinkles in your brain to get hard and gray, more like desert-scorched ruts. And ruts and graves differ only in degrees of length and depth. Grandma used to say, "Do something twice and you've got yourself a habit that'll take two dozen tries to break." That's if we *want* to change our habits. Fear nails our neurons to the floor. We'll understand better why when we have finished this book.

For now, trust that you are absolutely free to access another part of your brain, the right-sided Yin Mind. It just takes practice with some tips we'll find in a later chapter. Lo and behold, you will find yourself in possession of a Holy License To Fool With The Recipe. The wrinkles on your brain will soften up again and take on a softer hue and be more like breeze-chased ripples on the face of a serene and mysterious pond.

Your mind is truly soul-born and spirit-like. But when it shows up for work in your crusty old brain, just having come out of the slippery ether of a night's dreaming, it is woozy and knuckles under too easily to the Ego that's hard-wired into the machinery of your brain, the infamous Left Brain.

Your ego is one of those old-fashioned bosses who yells and threatens. The Big Intimidator. But what we will learn is how to silence the ego and direct your mind to do a balance of business in both hemispheres of the brain.

But we've got to have a revolution first. You know, overthrow the tyrant. We will have to do it with gusto and, if it seems we are a bit overzealous in our praise of our daring knight, the Right Brain and its Yin Mind workings, well, revolutions historically work that way. But after the fireworks things will settle down and be better than ever.

I invited you to be a doubter. So take me on. Do you even have a Right Brain, much less a herd of Yin Mind ponies ready to romp and play, dumping new and marvelous insights at your feet?

Sure, you've seen that little rift down the middle of brains in photos and the biology lab jars. And that makes it look like there's clearly a left side and a right side, but maybe that crease is only skin deep, as they say.

Thankfully, you don't need to pry open your lid and have a look. It's already been done. A Persian proverb says: "It is ignorance to test that which has already been tested." And since we are not ignorant, we'll pry open a book and have a look.

Three

"LEFTY TIGHTY, RIGHTY LOOSEY"*

*Actually, the phrase is "lefty loosey, righty tighty" and refers to which way to turn a nut on a bolt (or the lid on the jelly jar, for that matter) to tighten or loosen it.

Betty Edwards thinks there is a right brain. And she presents a pretty airtight case in favor of one: She teaches people to draw whose entry-level artistic skills are seriously lacking; one might even say impaired. Betty is the author of *Drawing on the Right Side of the Brain*, and she describes the basic premise of her book this way: ". . . drawing is a teachable, learnable skill," adding that anyone can draw "by gaining access to the part of your mind that works in a style conducive to creative, intuitive thought. . . ."

To make her promise convincing, Betty has presented several of her students' before and after drawings done six weeks apart. The "before" attempts are third-grade-quality squiggles. The "after" drawings are beautifully rendered, some almost photographic, and were done only *six weeks later.*

Betty bolsters right brain theory with some provocative findings from "split-brain" studies carried out about twenty years ago by Roger W. Sperry and others at Cal Tech. From Betty's book: "The investigation centered on a small group of individuals who came to be known as the *commissurotomy,* or 'split-brain' patients."

The patients were persons greatly disabled by epileptic seizures involving both hemispheres of their brains. As a last resort the incapacitating seizures were controlled by means of an operation, performed by Phillip Vogel and Joseph Bogen. The connecting cable of nerve fibers between the two hemispheres, the corpus callosum, was severed surgically, thus isolating one hemisphere from the other.

"The operation yielded the hoped-for result: the patients' seizures were controlled and they regained health. In spite of the radical nature of the surgery, the patients' outward appearance, manner, and coordination were little affected; and to casual observation their ordinary daily behavior seemed little changed."

Now, for the first time, here were a group of people who literally had a left brain and a right brain. So, being the good scientists, Sperry and the Cal Tech could not pass up the opportunity to check out the truth of left- and right-brain thinking. They came up with a series of ingenious and subtle tests that revealed the reality of "hemisphere specialization," surprising new evidence that "each hemisphere, in a sense, perceives its own reality or, perhaps better stated, perceives reality in its own way."

The results from one test, to me, were just incredible. Patients were shown two different pictures, which were flashed quickly on a screen and in such a way that each hemisphere, then, received *different* pictures. The left eye saw a picture of a spoon and, because of the cross-over effect, the spoon image went to the right brain. The right eye saw a picture of a knife, which went to the left brain.

I know personally that the left brain processes most of the verbal skills. My mother had an aneurysm that ruptured in the left hemisphere of her brain, and she lost her ability to speak. Although she is otherwise healthy, and it's been three years since the stroke, she can still say only yes and no, okay, and one other four-letter word—an expletive that we'll delete.

I know, too, that the cross-over stuff is correct because my mother also lost the use of most of the right side of her body.

Back to Sperry and the split-brain patients who saw the spoon and knife pictures: Now if the researchers wanted to get at the information in the left brain, all they had to do was ask the patient to *name* what he saw. Naming is a verbal skill, and therefore left-brain functioning. The

31

"confidently articulate left hemisphere" caused the patient to say "knife" when quizzed about what he saw.

Now, if we wanted to get at the image in the right brain, all we'd have to do is ask the patient to reach behind a curtain with his left hand (right hemisphere) and pick out what had been flashed on the screen. The curtain is obviously to keep the eyes out of the game. The group of objects back of the curtain included a spoon and a knife. Remember, the right brain saw a spoon, and, sure enough, that is what the patient's left hand picked up.

If the left-brain, right-brain stuff is true, we should be able to create some real confusion between the hemispheres. All we have to do is ask the patient to *name* what he is holding in his hand. The verbal left brain has already said it saw a knife, and without the benefit of "seeing" what the hand behind the curtain is holding, tells researchers there is a knife in his hand.

Sure enough, "the right hemisphere, knowing that the answer was wrong but not having sufficient words to correct the articulate left hemisphere, [and not willing to give up the contest] continued the dialogue by causing the patient to mutely shake his head. At that, the verbal left hemisphere wondered aloud, 'Why am I shaking my head?'

"As a result of these extraordinary findings over the past fifteen years, we now know that

despite our normal feeling that we are one person,
a single being, our brains are double, each half
with its own way of knowing, its own way of
perceiving external reality.

"In a manner of speaking, each of us has two
minds, two consciousnesses, mediated and inte-
grated by the connecting cable of nerve fibers
between the hemispheres." (My bold-face italics.)

Betty Edwards then *proves* right-brain artistic
functioning by getting people who proudly
confess to a total lack of art talent to draw beautiful pictures. Basically, she says the artist is there in
us all, alive and well in the right brain. She knows
that if we can write legibly, then we possess the
motor skills required to accomplish a good,
detailed drawing. Think about what fine pen or
pencil control is demonstrated in merely writing
your name in a handsome, cursive style. Far and
away more difficult than drawing a nose.

What's going on, then, when we cannot draw
well? Our Right Brain artist is knuckling under to
the Left Brain art critic, who is yelling raucously
that the person we just tried to draw looks like a
frog hit by an eighteen-wheeler. Here is the
beauty of the Betty Edwards method: If what she
believes about the artist-in-residence in the right
brain is true, all she need do is present the intellect with a task that the left hemisphere art critic
will boycott.

So, if I ask you to draw a vase without looking
at the paper, your left brain virtually screams that

it will have nothing to do with it, will not allow its name to be signed to such foolishness. For all practical purposes, the left brain takes a hike. That leaves the artist in charge.

Your own Picasso-like genius gets to take over, too, for instance, if you are asked to draw an image that is represented upside-down. The left brain detests disorder and these weird instructions seem irrational and chaotic. But your right brain loves a little tomfoolery.

The effect of such a nontraditional approach to learning is to break down the mental barrier set up to keep your imagination and creativity on the back of the bus. In a short time, your artist will gain confidence and refuse to listen to the pinch-mouthed art critic. Then you can draw things right-side-up and any other way.

I know it sounds far-fetched, but prove it by the pudding. Look at the drawings on pages 11, 12 and 13 and others like them scattered throughout Betty's book. They are incredible testimonies of the presence in us all of, if not a Right Brain, then an incredible power of mind with talent beyond all our imaginings.

And we have only just begun to stir this cauldron. The truth about what you can do is just beginning to rise, like a savory, peppery steam curling upward from a fat black pot somewhere down in the Louisian bayou, where alligators grow long and mean and good gumbo is king of the table.

Four

"AUTHORITY! IS THERE AN AUTHORITY IN THE HOUSE?"

In a little sidebar, near the section in *Drawing on the Right Side of the Brain* where Betty Edwards presents the work of Roger Sperry, she gives us a quote from Sperry in a paper he published called "Lateral Specialization of Cerebral Function in the Surgically Separated Hemispheres." Said Sperry: "The main theme to emerge . . . is that there appear to be two modes of thinking, verbal and nonverbal, represented rather separately in left and right hemispheres, respectively, and that our educational system, as well as science in general, tends to neglect the noverbal form of intellect. *What it comes down to is that modern society discriminates against the right hemisphere.*" [Italics added.]

37

Now watch as the courage rises in this author and he adds what *he* thinks, which is contrary to the quote from the Weighty Authority.

It's not the right hemisphere of the brain that is being discriminated against. It is Yin Mind, which is usually *processed* in the right brain. *But it does not originate there!* Any more than your favorite sitcom originates in the picture tube of your television. If you believe in the notion of a soul, this ought not be too hard to swallow. Just put mind "out there" with soul.

I say that Yin Mind is *usually* processed in the right hemisphere, because studies have shown that when one hemisphere is damaged, the remaining hemisphere can assume the lost functions; the younger the person, the more likely it is that the adaptation will occur. Young soldiers who suffer brain trauma in battle are notable examples. So with only a left hemisphere you would still have the capacity for Yin Mind. But your mind—the yin and yang of it—exists *outside* the brain.

Think of it like this: your brain and body are the servant of your thoughts. For instance, when you have a thought of fear, the thought has no mass or weight, no color—nothing. A thought is real, but it is also definitely nonmaterial. Now the magic occurs: nonmaterial is transformed into material. Nonstuff becomes stuff when a thought of fear becomes metabolized into adrenalin. Alchemy enough to make Merlin jealous!

But even that is kid stuff compared to the

mystery of quantum mechanics, the science of subatomic phenomena.

A quantum physicist would tell you that *none* of your body parts is even solid since atoms are made of impulses of energy and intelligence, *not solid particles.* It is true, albeit almost as incomprehensible and troubling as looking up toward the stars in the night sky and thinking there is no end, or that there is an end. Our body is actually an energy system, which is in a constant state of flux. We are literally born again each second of our existence as atoms are exchanged for other atoms.

If we could do a freeze-frame on all this quantum activity and, like marine biologists tagging seals, mark every atom in a human body, we'd find every one replaced in just over a year. Radio isotope studies prove it. So body growth is not a function of "stretching." Bone, organ, and tissue cells and molecules are actually replaced to create a new and different form.

The brain can only *participate* in this process; it cannot *originate* the process, for it, too, is constantly being remade in an image and likeness that resides not in DNA but in the mind of God, or whatever you want to call the Original Cause. Could we say, "In the beginning was the Word" and that the real You, your deepest Self, is a whisper of energy and information from the Mind of the Universe?

A neurosurgeon can find the precise location in the brain where messages to, say, move the hand are "written." But no amount of digging has ever found or can ever find the writer of the message.

Say aloud, "I have a hand." Slow your thoughts and try to identify the "I" that has just spoken. It is not your brain that has the hand. "I have a brain" gets behind that mirror. "I have a thought" peeks behind that mirror. Behind all the mirrors of thought is the thinker of the thoughts, and that is You.

This notion—that the mind has a brain and not the other way around—is of course not new, not some incense-and-crystal-induced New Age philosophy. It is, as we said, simply putting the mind out there in the same ether where most people place the soul. In fact, I agree with those who view the mind as nothing less than the animating force of the human machine.

It seems less far-fetched when we admit that you can "make up your mind" to kill the body. And do so without ever lifting a finger. Loring T. Swain, MD, tells in his book *Arthritis, Medicine and the Spiritual Laws* that "A middle-aged married woman was admitted to the hospital because of acute pain in her right side below her ribs. It was diagnosed as a gall bladder condition that needed operation. While I was examining her she said calmly and with finality, 'I will not survive this operation.'

". . . I tried to reassure her by relating stories of the many gallbladder operations which had been performed successfully. She seemed satisfied. Her gallbladder was removed. It was found to be congested, but there were no stones and no evidence of malignancy. Her postoperative recovery was uneventful. . . . Yet ten days later, when the stitches were taken out, she began to fail.

"In spite of everything we did to save her, she died. The autopsy showed no physical cause for her death. . . .

"This experience convinced me that there was much to be learned about the power of the mind over the body and that many things in medical practice could not be explained on a purely physical basis."

You can also "make up your mind" to save the body. Fundamentalist religious practices that include snake handling and snake *bites* also include drinking pure strychnine, either of which is supposed to make you quite dead. When rattlesnake venom or poison drunk from a fruit jar has no effect on even one enraptured member of a congregation in full Pentecostal tilt, the door has been swung open on some heavy-duty mind over matter. Simpler examples include people waiting until after some special event, like a birthday or anniversary, before dying.

In Colin Wilson's *The Occult* he describes the attempt by the wealthy Prince Yussupov to kill Rasputin, giving him cyanide-poisoned cakes and wine. (Wilson also allowed that Rasputin seems to possess the peculiar quality of inducing shameless inaccuracy in everyone who writes about him.)

"The cyanide, which should have rendered him unconscious within a minute and killed him in four, seemed to have no effect. Yussupov shot him, too. But when he came back with other conspirators for the body, Rasputin got up, and burst through a locked door into the courtyard. He was shot again and then battered with an iron bar. Finally, he was dropped into the river through a hole in the ice. When his body was recovered, it was found he had died of drowning." The autopsy also showed no poison in the body.

Wilson believes Yussupov was probably lying about giving him the poison in the first place. But maybe old Ras' put it the same place the snakehandlers do. William James said it only takes "one white crow to prove all crows are not black." If not in Rasputin, then among the snakehandlers there is at least one white crow. Others roost among spontaneous remissions from cancer. *Spontaneous?* I can assure you nothing about the retreat of death "happens or arises without external cause." Life is ordained.

If I could put my hands on your original recipe, so to speak, and come up with a precise list of ingredients right down to the subatomic phenomena that glue it all together and go down to the local market and buy all the stuff, there would still be no way to stir all that carbon and oxgen and hydrogen and mercury and nickel and such into any kind of stew that would be *you.* It would remain a stew—better yet, that gumbo we've mentioned—of *stuff*. It would not be able to get up and walk down the street.

Roger Penrose, eminent physicist and Oxford professor of mathematics who shares with Stephen Hawking (*A Brief History of Time*) the prestigious Wolf Prize, took a turn with the mind-body question in *The Emperor's New Mind*. His book is heavy, as you might guess, but some of its lightest, albeit most provocative lines come when he plays with the idea of teleportation. You know, *Star Trek*'s "Beam me up, Scotty." Except with this "new and improved" teleporter, you don't disassemble Captain Kirk and reassemble him where he wants to go; you, in effect, fax him.

You scan and digitize the information in every toe, hair, muscle, cell, synapse, atom, and electron, then ship the data off at the speed of light via an electromagnetic beam to some distant planet. At the other end, as with a fax, you make a precise duplicate of the traveler "together with all his memories, his intentions, his hopes and his deepest feelings. At least, that is what's expected, for every detail of the state of his brain has been faithfully recorded, transmitted and reconstructed."

"Assuming that the mechanism has worked," Penrose muses, "the original copy of the traveler can be safely destroyed. Of course, the question is: 'Is this really a method of traveling from one place to another, or is it merely the construction of a duplicate together with the murder of the original?' Suppose it is true that the teleporter does actually work in the sense that the traveler's own awareness is actually reawakened in the copy of himself on the distant planet. . . . What would happen if the original copy of the traveler were not destroyed as the rules of the game demand? Would his awareness be in two places at once?"

If this is where the shoe has fallen, so to speak, let me drop another shoe, like it, right beside it: With a set of down-to-the-atom-precise scales, what kind of pounds-and-ounces evidence could we come up with for the departing soul. You already know the answer: none. A quantum analysis of your dead body would reveal not even one quark or electron missing. Parts intact, the cord has been yanked on your TV set.

Milan Kundera, in his novel *The Unbearable Lightness of Being,* said that the fundamental human experience is the seemingly irreconcilable duality of body and soul, though soul, he admits, is for some "nothing more than the gray matter of the brain in action." For those who think this way, *poof! I'm dead!* is all there is. It's a Yang Mind perspective, since yang requires hard evidence, which neither physicians nor physicists can provide.

But Yin Mind knows that when the rooster and all its feathers lie limply at the fox's feet, Chanticleer's cock-a-doodle-doo is still out there somewhere, still stirring the bright, crisp air of an eternal dawn. In fact, a bigger dose of Yin Mind can make you, too, fairly crow with exuberance.

But what does it take to coax your brain (and we can say Right Brain, if you like) to process more of Yin Mind? And will you be risking the loss of what precious mental ground you've gained all these years?

To the latter question: It's *balance* we seek. Paul's advice in his epistle to the Romans to "be ye transformed, therefore, by the renewing of your mind" might be better said by replacing *renewing* with *balancing.* "To each thing there is a season and a time for every purpose under Heaven" speaks of the need for balance. Yin and yang in balance turns the wheel of understanding.

When Emerson said that a foolish consistency is the hobgoblin of little minds, *he did not say consistency is foolish.* He and I and you all know we must fuel and replenish our body's fluids with consistency or the machine will perish. I want you to consistently stay on your side of the road and not meet me head-on at sixty miles an hour.

But I admit that, "revolution-style," I am overselling Yin Mind. The discrimination against intuitive, nonverbal intellect Roger Sperry spoke of weighs a ton. We are trying to break inertia here. There is much at stake, and the value to us as individuals and as a group sharing the same small spaces is fundamentally important.

Robert Pirsig put it this way in his book *Lila:* "With the identification of static and Dynamic

Quality [his capitalization] as the fundamental division of the world, Phaedrus felt that some kind of goal had been reached . . . ." Perhaps a bridge between primitive mysticism and quantum mechanics. Pirsig, in the person of his main character Phaedrus, declared that his own radical bias caused him to think of Dynamic Quality alone and neglect static patterns of quality: "Until now he had always thought that these static patterns were dead. They have no love. They offer no promise of anything. To succumb to them is to succumb to death, since that which does not change cannot live."

But Phaedrus knew that life can't exist on Dynamic Quality alone. Static patterns preserve our world. They prevent a state of continuous chaos and provide a necessary stabilizing force, protecting dynamic progress from deterioration.

But proceed with extreme caution: "Static quality patterns are dead when they are exclusive, when they demand blind obedience and suppress Dynamic change. . . . Neither static nor Dynamic Quality can survive without the other."

So what Emerson begged for in his essay *Self Reliance* was to not be consistent to a foolish degree. There's a true story that illustrates the point well. Putting my own spin on it, it goes like this: Jon shows up early at the clock factory one morning, quickly making his way to his office back in Research and Development. He's had a couple of nice wine-and-cheese evenings with the boss's secretary, so she pulls a string to get Jon in to see the boss.

"Oh, look, Boss. I stayed late last night and found a way, cleverly using quartz crystal and a battery, to move clock hands around the dial. Just think, no more mainspring. What do you think?"

"That you need to spend less time with such idle foolishness. We are the Swiss. And the Swiss know clocks . . . better than Bo knows football. This is a toy, and we don't have time for games. Get back to work!"

The Boss later felt badly for having been so tough on Jon. To help assuage Jon's dismay, he allowed him to go to the international trade show on the company credit card and gave him permission to display his toy on the table.

"Ah, so. What we have here?" asked the nice young man, inspecting the wares on Jon's table.

"Only a toy," said Jon, and explained just how the plaything worked.

"And was it difficult to acquire international patents?"

"Oh, we didn't bother."

"Ah, so," said the nice young man, absent-mindedly brushing lint from his lapel as he steppped backward, before turning to sprint from the expo hall.

And, so, the Swiss *gave* the Japanese the technology for quartz clock movements. In your wheelbarrow-load of books be sure to include reports of the decimation of the Swiss economy following this archetypal example of a foolish consistency. Don't get yourself stuck in it-don't-get-no-better'n-this Yang Mind. Let a can of Pringles remind you that all potato chips don't come home with several of their lot crumbled in the bottom of the bag.

Emerson's *Self Reliance* goes to the heart of Yin Mind. Since most of us only know part of one sentence, here is a little more of it:

"A foolish consistency is the hobgoblin of little minds, adored by little statesmen and philosophers and divines. With consistency a great soul simply has nothing to do. He may as well concern himself with his shadow on the wall. . . . Else if you be a man speak what you think today in words as hard as cannon balls, and tomorrow speak what tomorrow thinks in hard words again, though it contradict everything you said today. Ah, then, exclaim the aged ladies, you shall be sure to be misunderstood! Misunderstood! It is a right fool's word. Is it so bad then to be misunderstood? Pythagoras was misunderstood, and Socrates, and Jesus, and Luther, and Copernicus, and Galileo, and Newton, and every pure and wise spirit that ever took flesh. To be great is to be misunderstood."

Women, Mr. Emerson, might misunderstand the masculine bias you exhibit, but your positive intent cannot be misunderstood: Open your mind to change, to daring some inconsistency, and thereby risk becoming great.

Five

YIKES! IT'S A BOOK OF LISTS

If Yin Mind is inconsistent and dynamic, as opposed to static, what else is it? What are some of its other dare-me-to-be-great secret ingredients? In order to tell you, I have to declare war.

A musty old Greek philosopher by the name of Heracleitos (the Weeping Philosopher) went on about his doctrine of *polemos* ("war"), where he saw all reality in an exalted metaphysical principle of conflicting opposites: hot/cold, day/night, beginning/end, sound/silence . . . an *ad infinitum* piecemeal pairing of all human sensory experience. This was in about the fifth century before Christ.

At about the same time, another Greek philosopher, Parmenides, found the basis for his brand of Dualism in the radical opposition between the world of human sense experience and ultimate reality. He allowed that above all the multiplicity of opposing things there is ultimately the One (which, for most of us, is God). All duality for Parmenides, then, was merely an *illusory* fragmentation of the One brought about by the inherent limitations of human sensory experience.

Yin (literally, "the sunny side of the hill") and Yang (you guessed it), as canons of Chinese philosophy, were introduced in the fourth century B.C. in an appendix to the *I Ching,* or *The Book of Changes.* Here, too, the world we know is divided into pairs of opposites.

You can see how everybody was latching onto the same dualistic world view. Our senses literally depend upon contrary experience as a basis for perception. To be meaningful, sweet requires salty, hard requires soft, light requires dark and on and on and on and on in a vice versa way. And, yes, male requires female and female requires male in at least the most basic of ways.

What is beautiful in yin and yang is the belief that the one *requires* the other, and, in some small measure, *contains* the other. Within the ocean of your sleeping mind is a tiny island of wakefulness; on the vast plain of your wide-awake mind rises a single spire of daydreaming.

The symbol for yin and yang—like black and white commas intertwined—is a visual poem. The head of the dark half forms and describes the tail of the light half; the head of the light half forms and describes the tail of the dark half; and in this way the static image accomplishes the illusion of turning. Within the dark half's absence of all color is a small circle of light; within the light half's harmony of all colors is a small dark circle. Each contained within the other. From separation, fluid unity, contained within a circle, "the holiest of all symbols."

Black Elk, medicine man of the Oglala Sioux, said ". . . the Power of the World always works in a circle, and everything tries to be round. The sky is round and I have heard that the earth is round like a ball. And so are all the stars. The wind in its greatest power whirls. Birds make their nests in a circle, for theirs is the same religion as ours." No more perfect, or beautifully simple, symbolic representation of an idea exists than the circular and flowing yin and yang.

What is not beautiful is how lopsided we have become in favor of Yang Mind. It is poetical, to me, that yang is represented by the number nine and yin by the number six in the *I Ching.* Yin asks for less. In our wild-eyed, tongue-lolling sprint for more and bigger—you name it—we have become blind to the peace "less is more" can offer, to an end to the war of dualing opposites.

Remember, it is *balance* we seek when we set about to tweak our brains to develop more Yin Mind. We will not unkindly nor foolishly abandon Yang Mind—we need it the way we need consistency in right measure and at the right time.

But what is it about Yin Mind that arouses suspicion and discrimination on the one hand and yet dares me to be great on the other?

For some answers, let's take a look at a couple of lists.

Parallel Ways of Knowing

—J. E. Bogen,
"Some Educational Aspects
of Hemisphere Specialization"

left brain—right brain
intellect—intuition
convergent—divergent
digital—analogic
secondary—primary
abstract—concrete
directed—free
propositional—imaginative
analytic—relational/holistic
lineal—nonlineal
rational—intuitive
sequential—multiple
objective—subjective
successive—simultaneous

I Ching—the Book of Changes

Yin—Yang
feminine—masculine
negative—positive
moon—sun
darkness—light
yielding—aggressive
left side—right side
warm—cold
autumn—spring
winter—summer
unconscious—conscious
emotion—reason

Ponder the seeming incongruities of *moon, warm, autumn,* and *winter* appearing together in yin, and yang's *sun, cold, spring,* and *summer.*

Now let's stir both these lists into our pot of gumbo. Easy does it. Don't slosh anything out— not yet, that is. Let it all simmer as we continue our own list, exploring the qualities of Yin Mind and Yang Mind.

WORDS❂SYMBOLS

My mother can no longer speak following a left-brain stroke, so I may conclude that her verbal skills were being processed in the left hemisphere. Words are a Yang Mind function.

The Oriental languages are written with characters, not letters: a fish has its very own symbol, a dog another one, the moon another, etc.—no fewer than 15,000 symbols to learn if you want to write fluently in Chinese. We, on the other hand, learn 26 letters, put an F beside an I followed by an S and an H which makes a word and the word becomes the symbol for fish.

If you think about it, words are symbols for feelings, things, concepts, etc., and the words themselves are made up of symbols (letters). A word is then twice removed from reality. Further, is "cold" the temperature outside or the ache in my sinuses? I could go crazy here and say that cold, in either case, is only a symbol for the underlying quantum physical circus that leads to the condition "cold" and the word is not twice but *three* times removed from ultimate reality. Is it any wonder we have so much trouble really communicating?

Back to naming the parts of our world . . . . If things weren't crazy enough already, when Yang Mind is finished making the word, look out for the fireworks when Yin Mind gets hold of those words. Yinned-out poets begin to mold them into things which they are not, but *could* be if you think about it just right.

"Jane is a lion."

No she is not. She is a woman who behaves metaphorically like a lion. Metaphors work well to describe some quality that Jane has—her aggressive business skills or what-have-you—by creating a picture in the mind of the reader. Then art can happen: the artist and his audience have become interactive. Images and impressions of all the lion experiences the reader has ever had, real or imagined, rush in to transform Jane, painting her into a beautifully complex person.

But metaphors take the Liar's Prize. Jane does not chase down antelopes and rip their throats out. But we're missing the point to say that cirro-cumulus is the truth, so to speak, and a hippo-potamus playing there in the sky is a lie.

Yin Mind is Poet's Mind. Philosophers into the yin of things like to take their turn with the

concept of metaphors, too, like Goethe, who said
that all reality—including people—is a metaphor.
That's heavy. But not unique. Other poet-philoso-
pher types have said this is all God's dream, that
he is dreaming us and we are dreaming each other
and, furthermore, that we may *direct* the dream.
Before things get too fuzzy, what we may know
about dreams with a modicum of certainty is that
the endowment of most of us with a dreaming
mind proves that imagination is among mankind's
deepest needs.

If I asked you to take the verbal data compart-
mentalized and categorized in your Yang Mind
and become a poet, a philosopher, to play a
metaphors game with me, would you be able to
shake loose from a narrow literal use of words?
Could you escape the tendency toward an old saw
and think up an original metaphor, say, for a
mother's love? What would you choose?

Now we aren't talking about similes, where
you say something is *like* something else. We're
talking about the whole get-out-of-your-ordinary-
mind poetical approach. "A mother's love is the
rain in spring, falling lazily—" Insert here the
sound of a loud irritating buzzer and an
announcer's voice saying in a conciliatory manner, "Thanks so much for playing the game, but
that is really trite."

Toni Morrison, this country's seventh Nobel
laureate in literature, on the other hand, takes the
prize in our metaphors game when she compares

a mother's love to syrup. *Syrup?* Yes. In this way:

It didn't take long, after Jude left, for her to see what the future would be. She had looked at her children and knew in her heart that that would be all. That they were all she would ever know of love. But it was a love that, like a pan of syrup kept too long on the stove, had cooked out, leaving only its odor and a hard, sweet sludge, impossible to scrape off. For the mouths of her children quickly forgot the taste of her nipples, and years ago they had begun to look past her face into the nearest stretch of sky.

The book reviewer for *Playboy* said Toni Morrison's *Sula* (from which the foregoing was taken) is "written in language so pure and resonant that it makes you ache." The *Detroit Free Press* wrote: " . . . such tone and grace and wisdom that the effect is almost hypnotic." And Yin Mind is the hypnotist. Writers might call it The Muse. It matters no more, however, what we call *it* than where we imagine *it* is located. Yang Mind is the keeper of vocabulary and the rules of grammar. Yin Mind is employed as the poet who transforms the dictionary and do's and don'ts of good language skills into literary art that holds and speaks and molds the very soul of the society which it reflects.

It was Yin Mind that put the phrase "zero at the bone" onto the page for Emily Dickinson when she set about describing a meeting with a snake, a "narrow fellow" in the grass. Yang Mind would say that the temperature of one's bones does not vary according to emotional states. Yin Mind delights, however, in conveying the experience of fear to readers with a turn of phrase like "zero at the bone."

One of my writing teachers told me the biggest deterrent to good writing is to interrupt the creative flow by letting the editor in our head step in and say this is no good. Editing is yang; writing is yin. In his "Peanuts" cartoon strip, Charles Schulz illustrated the concept beautifully. At the opening of the strip Lucy is kicked back at her desk behind a sign that says "Editorial Queen." Snoopy, sitting on his dog house, has typed: "Suddenly a shot rang out."

Lucy asks to see what he's written so far, takes the page from Snoopy, scans it with furrowed brow and says, "You know it's very important to select the perfect words . . . in this case I wonder if 'suddenly' is the right word?"

Snoopy takes back his page, ponders a moment while gazing at the clouds, then types: "Gradually a shot rang out." And that kind of ruination happens when we let Editor Yang step in too quickly on our creative endeavors. That same screechy voice would scare you away from putting in more hot sauce than the gumbo recipe calls for. Or telling the boss your suggestions for innovation to "business as usual."

Further illumination of the process comes from an article by Alan Blackburn that appeared several years ago in *Writer's Digest* entitled "Fast-Write." Seems Alan's dad hired him to help with some press releases and paid him by the page—the faster he ground out the pages, the more he earned. Said Alan: "The event to bring Fast-Write into full bloom happened one hot morning in July. I sat typing with sweat dribbling into my eyes. This was back in the good old days when we endured without air conditioning. I was struggling to make it as a writer. I had graduated from Harvard with honors in English. But there was a catch. I couldn't write. More precisely, I couldn't write anything that anyone would buy."

As Alan wrote faster and faster he " . . . became gradually aware of a curious phenomenon. Words and phrases over which I had no control poured directly to my fingers from somewhere in my head. My brain was dictating to me. The words it led me to punch out rated in quality far above any conscious effort of mine." That part about "conscious effort" is a tip-off. Yin Mind is *un*conscious and way outside the brain.

That did it. Alan guessed the secret of creative writing lay deep in some fold of his brain that he was not aware of. "I hied to the public library and signed out all the books on brain research I could lay my hands on. . . . I had been granted a vision of what brain power, residing just below the level of awareness can do . . . ."

After going on for a bit in the article about brain research, Alan assures readers who hope to write better that they need not "bone up for a Ph.D. in brain science."

Most experts, he said, agree that right and left halves of the brain work as a team in two different modes: a fast, *natural* mode, and a slow, logical mode. The natural mode is creative, spontaneous, relaxed, timeless, and intuitive. The logical mode is critical, rational, tense, and guiltily *self*-con-scious.

"Make friends with *both* modes," Alan advises. "Natural mode gives birth. Logical mode cleans up baby. Natural is effortless; logical is labored. Natural writes; logical edits." And the rest of the article is a how-to for pokey writers who, in writing faster, will tap into the right-brain natural mode.

Another how-to piece in another issue of *Writer's Digest* offered a high-tech way to get creative by hooking yourself to an electronic "brain machine." The reporter tested one of these devices and told of others. The gadget he wore generated a pattern of flashing LEDs in a pair of opaque glasses worn over the eyes. A stereo headset transmitted a tone synchronized with the lights stimulating the brain to produce super-creative alpha and theta waves.

"On one occasion, I fell into a dream with pictures taking the places of the flashing lights. A song formed in my head and I could see the song being performed. Images grew from the song and spread out like waves across other images."

When the reporter's eight-year-old daughter tried the brain machine, she found herself "wandering within a video game. She saw rainbows and cities and other things she could not quite describe."

When I have asked my elderhostelers if they would try a "brain machine," the overwhelming majority say no. Maybe they are simply expressing a fear of the unknown. But I am all in favor of natural access to the creative wizard within you, and dubious of external stimulants, electronic or otherwise, to artificially enhance Yin Mind.

RULES◉FREEDOM

Some years back *National Geographic* did a story on alcoholism and somewhere in the body of the text they put a question: "Why is it that five of six (before Toni Morrison made it seven) Nobel Prize-winning authors in this country have been alcoholics?" The query suggests a relationship between alcohol and creativity.

Without a doubt. Yang Mind is an avowed rule keeper who wants nothing to do with imbibing more than a "respectable" couple of drinks. "I will not be present to witness such debauchery," says Yang, "and will take my leave of this carrying on." And when yang is away, yin will surely play. We are wide open for tomfoolery. You know better than to kiss the boss's husband, especially with your old man and the boss looking on! But you don't give a yin with yang out of town for the evening. Yin Mind is for sure brought into full bloom, not only with brain machines, but with garden variety hooch.

Or with the "herb": An Oglala Sioux medicine man setting out on a vision quest might follow the trail of smoke wafting from a communal toke; a Yaqui might munch peyote for a "broader view of reality"; Edgar Allen Poe might hear the beating of a tell-tale heart after a visit to the opium den.

A caution flag is raised (and a promise to tell you the one sure-fire way to access Yin Mind, drug-free, before we finish this book): Yin Mind is unmindful of rules and, without a balance of order from Yang Mind, may even take things into the realm of anarchy and chaos.

Mother Nature knows better than to let things get out of kilter. It's interesting to look at the relatively new thinking in science called Chaos Theory, which finds, even in seemingly totally random events—say footsteps on a tourist beach— patterns of order. Remember the mesage of the yin-yang symbol: within the blackness of chaos shines a small circle of order.

It is sad to me when creative genius plays too close to the edge of chaos. Alcohol- and/or drug-induced art, though brilliant, can also spell the annihilation of the artist, albeit—in many cases— with the artist's full knowledge and complicity. But whether Hemingway, Faulkner, Steinbeck, O'Neill, and Lewis (to the *Geographic's* question) drank first from a freewheeling yin attitude or the drunk chicken laid an egg oozing with the muse is a question we cannot answer. That Pearl Buck was not a drunk and the only woman in the first six Nobel laureates suggests at least a look at whether the female brain has a better natural link to Poet Mind.

We do get grandiose in our thinking when well oiled with hundred-proof. And imaginative grandiosity, not cautious reserve, is the stock in trade of truly creative people. Ernest Hemingway pulled out all the stops in *Islands in the Stream* when he wrote the exchange between Bobby the bartender and the artist Thomas Hudson.

Bobby, a bit incredulous that people would actually buy paintings of everyday life on the island, describes to Tom what *he* would buy in a painting. Bobby tells the artist in marvelous, hilarious, outlandish exaggeration of paintings of waterspouts ("Black as hell . . . God's own hell of a waterspout") and all manner of Nature's fury, tossing out a breathless: "Tom, boy, do you think you could paint a full hurricane?" Read those few pages in *Islands in the Stream* for a glimpse of Yin Mind unbridled, and some writing that would make Sam Clemens white-haired with envy.

Yin Mind in its tamer aspects is manifested in mild rule-breaking eccentricities of dress and behavior that spark a smile or turn heads on the sidewalk or makes the family blush at the Thanksgiving dinner table over the mention of Uncle Vester dumpster-diving again. I heard an unconfirmed story that Einstein wore the same clothes for the last ten or so years of his life. Michael Crichton, when he wrote *Jurassic Park,* had his character, Ian Malcolm, the mathematician, wear only black because it was a waste of mental energy to stand in front of a row of clothes trying to decide on the day's fashion statement.

When Yin Mind abandons the rules, it seems also to sometimes abandon memory as if it were a chief means by which rules reach their ends. When Emerson talked about self-reliance, he spoke of dragging about a "corpse of memory" lest we contradict ourselves.

Flights of whim and fancy are often accompanied by absent-mindedness. My wife would probably argue that I am guilty of a willful refusal to commit to memory things like taking out the trash on the right day without a reminder. To the former, I think of the story about Beethoven purchasing the milkman's horse to rescue it from a beating, then forgetting about the animal until he was told it starved to death; to the latter, the story of Einstein relying on the phone book for his home phone number, asking why he'd bother his mind—waste precious space in his case—with remembering something that could be so handily looked up.

At the other end of the stick from mild eccentricities are the ideas and behavior of the likes of Copernicus and Galileo and Pythagoras and Jesus—guys who were truly misunderstood, at least within the context of the social and scientific milieu of their day. But no matter the date, we are always suspicious of anyone who comes speaking for change.

Why does "nothing vex the priest like a saint in the congregation"? Because saints, in the course of putting on their pants like you and me (they get their saint stripes much later, all things being clearer with hindsight), challenge and threaten the status quo. Organized religion, if it hopes to remain organized, must ensure that its clergy defend the institution. But a saint is a loose cannon where canon is concerned.

Abraham Lincoln, who never became a member of the institutional church, said he'd join the one with a single rule to love all people. Lincoln was definitely a saint in the congregation of American politics. And got himself killed for it. So have many others who, like him, speak for fundamental change to the social landscape.

Our violent opposition to change and the agents of change is a terrible irony in the face of the reality of change. Change is the "only immutable law in the universe." Within change lie "pure potentiality" and the "field of all possibilities," the hope of something better.

Even old Newton's *laws* have had to move over for quantum physics' new *laws*, which will bend to other laws as they are discovered.

And there's nothing new with any of these discoveries, mind you. What is true has always been true. Change is the means available to human beings to evolve toward greater understanding of what is true. Change is the means of exchanging perception for knowledge.

Ultimate Reality is the ever-becoming—always the Tao's Uncarved Block. When you attempt to take a concept like God and chip it into the evanescent thing of your flawed perceptions, the object of your capricious cravings, it is theology destined for the yard sale. Truth is always an Uncarved Block. Although we may not ever file and shape Truth to suit our needs, we may approach an understanding of it when we open our minds to change. And, besides, we don't have to know the way to God—He knows the way to us.

It is only openness to fundamental change that we may rely on. So why can we not align ourselves more easily with change? Because of an imbalance of Yang Mind. It is the lord of static quality.

What's more, Yang Mind is too preoccupied with looking to see how much time we've got to allow us to become grounded in the very present moment . . . always exchanging itself for the present moment . . . and changing itself into the present moment . . . the ever-becoming present moment where time is in infinite supply.

TIME❀UNBOUNDED ETERNITY

Philosophers, poets, and physicists agree that time is an invention of humans, a consequence of our sensory perception, to compartmentalize our experiences. Time is a notion. The tick-tocking in our brains includes what has passed, what is now, and what is to come—past, present, and future.

Our linear model of time has it rolling ever forward from the now in an imaginary vehicle that has no reverse gear: the cup that falls and is broken never gets itself unbroken. Everybody can see that, but few look meaningfully at the fact that neither is there a forward gear in the sense that we cannot actually depart from the now by even one nanosecond into the "future." Even if we develop time travel, no matter where and when we go, there we will be—in *that* present moment.

So there is, in fact, only this very present moment. Yin Mind knows it well. Yin Mind knows, too, that the movement of time we perceive is not a phenomenon of chronology, but an experience of the present moment always becoming, translated through our perceptions into the metaphor we call time. That our *perceptions* are subject to doubt need go no further than our admission about the perception of the "flat, stationary" planet beneath our feet.

So when you "lose track of time," bet your bippy that you've made the shift to Yin Mind. See how easy it is, even in our culture's yang-infested waters, to find yourself effortlessly a-lounge on an island of boundless, eternal yin consciousness. When did it last happen to you? Were you washing dishes in the good old time-*consuming*, by-hand way, staring out the window, 'blivved-out (root word: *oblivion*) and unconcerned about *dead*lines. Then Yang-Father sternly addresses your consciousness: "Boy! The mall closes in thirty minutes and tomorrow's Mother's Day—"

But any time you are left alone, doing something you love to do, doing it in "the zone," you are processing the world through timeless Yin Mind. Of course sunbathing with a lovely, slightly attired him or her passes at warp speed, but so can your *job!* Do you think Joe Namath was watching the clock—even in a job where seconds count—when he quarterbacked his flawless Super Bowl, and said that he wasn't playing football, that football was playing him?

Notice that your right work is even necessary to spiritual growth. Here's Mr. Buddha's Noble Eightfold Path to Nirvana:

1. Right Understanding
2. Right Aspiration
3. Right Speech

4. Right Conduct
5. **Right Vocation**
6. Right Effort
7. Right Alertness
8. Right Concentration

You can't even get to Nirvana from here if you aren't in your right work. There is a saying, "Those who find a job they love never work again." It could also mean you won't ever again need to be alarmed out of a cozy and sound sleep in the morning.

The yin state is so unconscious of time it can make that long and boring drive to your in-laws fairly whiz by. Slipping into Yin Mind is as easy as slipping a good book-on-tape into the car's cassette player. An engaging "read" while driving will beam in a yin time warp every time. What's more, the yin state, which cares not a tinker's damn for cataloguing data—even big, important stuff—will lose whole cities from your awareness as you motor down the interstate. How we propel and guide that rolling rocketship down the highway in our right lane with Yin Mind at the wheel is an unsolved mystery.

A student at an elderhostel I taught told me that when she is in her studio painting she sometimes doesn't realize it's getting late until her stomach growls a reminder to her. In this case, her hunger is a little dot of yang time-sense in the curling yin comma of eternity.

Children are way Yin Mind dominant. Tell

your four-year-old to come inside in a few minutes for lunch. And where is she in a few minutes? I don't know, but she is not inside. Left alone, it will be little Amanda's own hungry belly (or black nightfall) that will ask her in.

Now this is gospel: if you are going to get this yin-yang stuff straight, in fact, you will probably have to become a child again.

ADULT☯CHILD

It caught on with some people when Jesus said let the children come to him, that unless we change and become like little children we'll never even darken the door of Heaven. The Apostle Paul, for one, liked the idea. In Romans 12:2 (New English Bible) he said "Adapt yourselves no longer to the patterns of this present world, but let your minds be remade and your whole nature thus transformed." Remade in the image and likeness of a child, I would add. Some of our finest essayists, from Emerson and Thoreau to Montaigne, rolled around this notion of the need for returning to our childlike natures.

Some of you who are damn' well certain there's no such thing as a yin and a yang but are pretty sure you've got a brain might still doubt whether that little crease down the middle of the thing really means you have a left brain and a right brain. If it vexes you, that's okay. The words are just talk that tries to make sense of the way we think. We could just as easily skip Left Brain, Right Brain, yin and yang, and talk about adult minds and child minds. A frolic back down memory lane to the mindscape of your childhood can teach us a lot.

Rainer Maria Rilke (1875–1926) was a German poet. If you have not read his poems, please do, particularly the one about hearts won back. Someone dear to me struggled to win back her heart, having put it at risk in an adolescent confusion of drugs and lies. Rilke suggests that those who have wandered into those dangerous places and found their way back are more blessed than those who stay at home. And, like the prodigal son, deserving of our love and forgiveness.

Especially, too, have a look at Rilke's *Letters to a Young Poet*, ten letters written to a young man seeking his advice on the writer's craft, letters as beautiful, at times, as any of his verse. It is more touching to know that Rilke himself had an unhappy childhood when you read his advice regarding which emotions are fit grist for the poet's mill: "Everything that you can think in the face of your childhood, is right."

Rilke also advised the young poet to think of his childhood, and ". . . if you think of your childhood you live among them again, among the solitary children, and the grown-ups are nothing, and their dignity has no value.

"And if it worries and torments you to think of your childhood and of the simplicity and quiet that goes with it, because you cannot believe any more in God, who appears everywhere in it, then ask yourself, dear Mr. Kappus, whether you really have lost God? Is it not, rather, that you have never possessed him?" No child has an interest in possessing God.

While territoriality is certainly a trait children possess, it is only lightly guarded and beautifully inconsistent. I watched through the window the other day as my little boy was about to trade his new pop gun for a roll of tart candies. We, too, must be willing to trade the God of our under-standing to a new understanding, realizing that God is not changing, He is simply drawing nearer to us.

But the yang-minded adult wants to capture long-white-whiskered First Cause within some formulation of dead rules. Jung said religious ritual is too often a defense against religious experience. God cannot be circumscribed, or *said*, which is why only polymorphous poetical com-ments from the mouth of a child even come close to describing God.

Jesus got himself in big trouble with the adults for suggesting it is the spirit of the law that is worth keeping, not its letter. Ask a kid if it's okay to run a red light if his puppy is in the back seat bleeding and needs to get to the vet.

And children are not into politically correct

varnishments. They will, as we know, tell the truth when we adults are more likely to withhold or rename it.

"Helga is a *heavyset* lady."

"Man, is she *fat*, or what?"

Yin Mind is Child Mind. We "big-boned" big people are merely fat to a kid.

But the refreshing honesty, simplicity, and myriad good qualities of our young ones are in jeopardy in our driven society. It is a testimony to the truth of Rilke's "and the grown-ups are nothing, and their dignity has no value" that we have not protected childhood for our children.

HEAD❧HEART

Tennessee Williams must have been out of his everloving mind when he essayed about "The Catastrophe of Success." How else could he have said that " . . . success is a kind of death, I think, and it can come to you in a storm of royalty checks beside a kidney-shaped pool in Beverly Hills."

But, wait—there's more:

"Once you fully apprehend the emptiness of a life without struggle, you are equipped with the basic means of salvation . . . that not privation but luxury is the wolf at the door and that the fangs of this wolf are all the little vanities and conceits and laxities that success is heir to—why then with this knowledge you are at least in a position to know where the danger lies."

And more:

"Then what is good? Obsessive interest in human affairs plus a certain amount of compassion and moral conviction . . . that must be translated into pigment or music or dance or poetry or prose or anything that is dynamic and expressive [including the living of your life, which is your *real* artwork]—that's what's good for you . . ."

Well, Mr. Williams *was* out of his head when he wrote this stuff. He was writing squarely from his heart, and the heart doesn't concern itself with money. Your heart is as good a candidate for the "true seat of the emotional, unconscious mind" as is the right brain or cerebellum. Ninth-grade science students know that "thinking" occurs at the cellular level and is not limited to the brain itself. Don't forget that your "*gut* feelings" are wonderfully wise!

A businessman I know told me he pays his employees to do things right, not to do the right thing. That's too bad. Too often, the common denominator within business management goes like this: "You have to do business—count the money and all that—with your head; keep your heart out of it. It's way too mushy for a good, solid bottom line. How can you stay in business if you give the man your pants when he only asked for your shirt? The margin of profit in these wolfish times comes down to *threads*, never mind whole garments."

Your heart answers back: "What good's the profit when your balance sheet lacks soul? Besides, God's got all the money, the pockets just change. If I always do the right thing by folks, my pocket will always have enough in it."

Your yang-minded head can hardly brook that kind of thinking. Head says money may not buy happiness but it sure pays the way while you are in hot pursuit. Heart says "success is a kind of death."

Yang wants stuff—yin is interested in people and ideas. Yang is object-referral—yin is self-referral. Deepak Chopra has helped to popularize this pair of opposites and uses a parable to illustrate the point: A farmer's horse runs away and his neighbor tells him how sorry he is to hear the news. The horse one day returns from its adventuring followed by a whole herd of wild mountain ponies; his neighbor comes to say, "Now, ain't that some good news!" But then the farmer's son falls while trying to tame the horses and breaks his leg. Here comes the neighbor to express his heartfelt sadness at the misfortune. The next day, however, the army comes through the village conscripting all the young men into service to help fight a bloody war that had broken out on the border. You guessed it, the farmer's son was allowed to remain safely at home.

Chopra explains how wild swings from elation

to sadness are the continuous plight of people who are trapped in an *object-referral* mode, who make reference to objects—including situations and circumstances—for a sense of well-being and happiness. Think of how *experience* rarely meets *expectations*. Real happiness doesn't come and go with the horses—or BMWs or royalty checks or crowd approval or a good-looking husband or a sweet wife or the neighborhood Yard of the Month sign. These things are good for flashes of pleasure with concomitant flashes of disappointment—"buyer's remorse." The horse runs away, the Beemer gets scraped in the parking lot, the check is in the mail, the people boo, the hunk cheats, the sweet wife gets PMS, and the landscaper's bill arrives.

Happiness is self-referral, intrinsic and oblivious of fame or shame. It blankets your psyche and keeps you warm and fuzzy regardless of whatever outrageous misfortune may spin your way. It is the scriptural peace that passes all understanding. Henry Miller said from a London jail cell that he had no money and no job, no prospects and no hope. " . . . I am the happiest man alive," he said.

That Henry included "no hope" in his list bugged me for a time until it occurred to me that hope, from one line of sight, could be seen as a future bet on better times than these and is, therefore, hardcore object-referral yang thinking. Jesus said he prayed not for our freedom *from* difficulties, but peace *within* difficulties.

It is interesting that I found Chopra using a parable to illustrate an object-referral state of mind that I first read in *Sadhana* by Anthony de Mello, SJ. De Mello used the same story to say that what seems to be good may turn out to be bad and what seems bad may turn out good. We should therefore leave it to God to decide what is good and bad and trust that, in time, all things *will* work out well for "those who love him."

At that level of trust we will share something of that marvelous mystical vision of Dame Julian of Norwich, who uttered the loveliest and most consoling sentence I have ever read: *"Sin is behovely, but all shall be well and all shall be well and all manner of thing shall be well."* This the heart knows, while the head forever doubts it.

The head is not bad. Let's not throw that baby out with the bathwater. Its yang tendencies toward consistency just need to be tempered with yin surprises from the heart. The head does a fine job keeping our *do-re-mi-fa-so-la-ti-dos* in perfect pitch, but let the heart write the melody.

Cut your heart loose, too, in the laboratory. It can be quite the scientist in all its wild imaginings. The head, lusting for *laws* of science, keeps the knowledge catalogued and orderly; it requires a point of reference for everything, including itself (the job description of our ego). But the heart's curiosity gives rise to flights of fancy that yield discoveries it sometimes takes the head years to *prove.*

79

Or, the heart figures out the answer to a heady problem . . . no, wait! Yin Mind doesn't *cipher*—it just *knows*, always. Problem is, of course, Yin Mind speaks with symbols, not words. Yang Mind is not fluent in the language of symbols, so it is sometimes slow to get the message.

Can't you just see the big-eyed kid with tousled hair in the dimly lit back corner of the classroom who is always thrusting his hand into the air, waving it, hoping the teacher will call on him? But she never does—until (quick, get the popcorn, the good part's coming) *one day* when not another child knows the answer and the teacher's about to have them all get down and do fifty push-ups or something. At the last minute she spots the little boy with his hand raised and *tah-dah!* The day is saved and all live happily ever after.

How long had Friedrich Kekule (1829–1896) been ignoring the pleading of his heart for a turn? He was a German chemist who laid the ground-work for modern structural theory in organic chemistry, up late nights in the laboratory, brushing back his hair with tired hands as he bends over his notes on the molecular structure of benzene, blinking back the blur that keeps clouding his vision until, "Well . . . maybe tomorrow."

Then (from *Encyclopaedia Britannica*): "One night in 1865 Kekule dreamed of the benzene molecule as a snake biting its tail while in whirling motion. From that vision his concept of the six-carbon benzene ring was born, and the facts of organic chemistry known up to that time fell into place." And you thought only fuzzy-headed mystic-types were into "visions." But Yin Mind *is* Dreaming Mind.

You could say that when you sleep your left-hemisphere brain dominance takes a break. There's nothing to categorize, analyze, compartmentalize, no need to keep track of time. So your left brain goes on hiatus, leaving your right brain in charge for a change, and it just goes nuts, scripting in picture language all those crazy dreams, piling them on the desk of your mind only to have your daytime yang-dominated consciousness swipe them into the morning trash, or not remember them at all. Or I could say your head goes to sleep and your heart, which must stay awake pumping anyway, runs the mind show for those few hours until morning.

Sometimes we turn over the reins of mind to heart in broad daylight. Einstein said he was *daydreaming*, "taking a ride on a beam of light" when he conceptualized relativity. Here's the ultimate math head having one of those "visions." Out of the ether comes the Theory (from the Greek word *thea*, "a vision") of Relativity. Then for fifty years Einstein's and hundreds of others' heads sweat bullets proving what one heart knew and delivered up teasing, easy-like, to a brain half-napping on an afternoon sofa.

From your wheelbarrow of books, read about

the dream doings of Robert Louis Stevenson, Samuel Taylor Coleridge, Nobel laureate Otto Loewi, Elias Howe, William Blake, Paul Klee, composers Mozart, Beethoven, Wagner, Tartini, and others, Jack Nicklaus (ten strokes off his game overnight), Ingmar Bergman, Judith Guest, and on and on. In fact, get Stephen LaBerge's book *Lucid Dreaming*, which has something to say about the folks we've just named. La Berge tells us that Kekule, on the occasion of presenting his dream discovery to his colleagues, said "Gentlemen, let us learn to dream."

Which is like Einstein's valuing imagination over knowledge. Which is like, learn to listen to your heart and cultivate a yin for change.

Six

QUICK, ETHEL, FETCH THE ALMANAC!

Okay, okay . . . enough with the paired opposites already. But, face it, this stuff never stops. Our flawed dualistic perception is an umbrella underneath which gathers our entire world. You can enlist the aid of your yang deductive reasoning skills to assign yin and yang positions for everything from "deductive/inductive," to aphorisms like: "look before you leap"/ "he who hesitates is lost."

All those maxims Grandma taught us are a fun list to look at because each maxim has its counter-maxim. And what's even more fun is the curious way that *both* maxims are true according to the verities of time and place. Think about the nature of reality that is suggested by opposite aphorisms each being true.

You don't need to pay to take the Hermann Brain Dominance Instrument to find out whether you are primarily of Yin Mind or Yang Mind; just make a long list of opposing maxims and see which list appeals most to your "way of thinking."

But if it's balance we seek to cultivate, and our yang clearly needs more yin, are there tips for the willing gardeners?

Yes, that's the good news and the impetus behind our little book. And it's worthwhile to begin with consideration of the time in our life when we first began to get so lopsided in our balance of yin and yang thinking.

Men can, I suppose, simply lay the blame on their brains. I just read this by Brad Lemley in the June issue of *New Age Journal*:

> Brain structure studies show that in women the corpus callosum—the part of the brain that connects the emotional right brain to the rational left brain—is a thick, dense sort of neuronal superhighway. Because the left brain is also the speech and writing center, women's emotions can essentially roar down the superhighway from inception to expression.
>
> A man's corpus callosum, conversely, is said to be less rich and dense with neurons. It has been described (by men's-movement gurus, for example) as a sort of dark, narrow, pot-holed street. This means that, while men's right brains may be churning out just as many emotions [and other

Yin Mind stuff] as are women's, these feelings face gridlock when trying to commute to the other side of the brain, where they could be released . . . The [emotions] are piling up in the right side of men's brains like four P.M. traffic at the Holland Tunnel. In defense of men, I'd like to point out that this is not necessarily bad.

Or—and don't take this personally, Brad, and the rest of you hardware-oriented souls—necessarily the reason for the pile-up. It's that old nature/nurture question again with the decision, this time, going to "the way we nurture our nature" for the yang imbalance, not the way the machine is wired.

Into your wheelbarrow toss John Gray's *Men are from Mars, Women are from Venus* and Daniel Goleman's *Emotional Intelligence*—and neither author(ity) necessarily agrees with me, in fact, and both tend to lean, instead, toward a "hardware versus software" read on the yin and yang of thinking. If you got all the books you could lay your hands on about male and female brain stuff, you'd need a second or third wheelbarrow—and that wouldn't be a bad idea.

Suffice it to say, guys (or gals), blaming our brain for the way we think is a big cop-out. Nurture your nature differently and find yourself thinking differently.

What about the "mentally challenged?" (Forgive me if this is not the politically correct label.) Their thought processes have seemingly built-in glitches. That is another and very long book which I will not write but which others have already. I will add only a couple of lines to those books: The human experience is not about fiscal or physical or intellectual stability—we become human to learn to love. Period. And dogs could teach MBAs and MDs, JDs and PhDs more than a thing or two about that. No one who observes brain function limitation can prove a concomitant limitation on the power and capacity for love. Even those whom psychologists label sociopaths or psychopaths can also love. The tree may be withered, but the roots still live.

So when did we begin to nurture an imbalance in our nature toward yang thinking? We started writing that into our psyches at about age two and had most of the text completed by about age nine, followed by the rest of our years in varying stages and degrees of editing the basic manuscript.

Sperry said, remember, that both our "eductional *system* [italics added], as well as science in general" tend to neglect the nonverbal form of intellect—what we have been calling Yin Mind. Since the educational system turned out the scientists, it's there we will look. First we have to define the parameters of the educational system from a General Systems Theory approach. That would have us include within the educational system not only professional educators, but also mothers and fathers and every person we have ever taken notice of in all our relationships in our culture and society, past and present. Within this system, aided and abetted by the corpse of our own memories and a yang disdain for change, we began as mere tots learning to engage in wholesale, big-lot purchases of Yang Mind stuff.

We send our children off to school, jarred from their soft dreams with a threatening: "Come on, get up. It's Monday and 6:30. Time to get ready for school. Hurry now! Let's not be late again today." But there is no such thing as Monday and 6:30 in the innocent reckoning of a child. She could ask, "What color is Monday, Daddy?"

But we teach them about time and sell them on the insane idea that it is in limited supply. We fashion for our children their very own set of boxes for putting the whole world into: Saturday is a hoot—Monday is hell. January's dreary—June's a dream. Boys: left—girls: right.

We teach our children far too hard the art of competition: A is for arrogant—D is for damaged, marked-down goods. If you aren't a jock you are a nerd. The developing Yang Mind's proudest accomplishment is an over-strong ego that wants at any cost to be "first." It will brook no challenges from humility. It can hijack all your emotions in a fraction of a second, having you kick the dog or kill the guy who cut you off on the interstate.

In *Emotional Intelligence* Dan Goleman blames these emotional hijackings on an almond-shaped cluster of brain structures called the amygdala. This is too hardware-oriented for me. The amygdala may indeed be the control stick, so to speak, but it is Yang Mind that is in the pilot's seat flying the warplane.

Yin Mind just kind of parachutes in later (sometimes, sadly, too late to prevent catastrophes), swinging on breaths that come slower and deeper, offering you a different perspective on events. Surveying the bombing site, yin thinking wonders: "Now why did I do that?"

But we aggressively educate our children toward yang intellectual, analytical competence while mostly ignoring yin emotional values like humility and generosity, and the cultivation of a positive regard for people with different ideas and characteristics from our own. We *don't* teach our children to admit that they might be wrong and that it is okay to say so. Balancing yin and yang for better conflict resolution might take three easy steps that a child could understand by first grade:

1. "I don't like the way I feel." (yang analysis)
2. "I might be wrong about this." (yin humility)
3. "Let's find a better way." (yin-yang balance)

But there's no need to continue repeating the obvious. You *know* how you were educated, at whose side, and what you have been taught. You *know* whether or not your learning has brought you a real measure of emotional peace and a real sense of security that will not fail you at the first brief encounter with the "slings and arrows of outrageous fortune."

If there *are* fragrant flowers everywhere in the garden of your well-taught mind, I believe you are blessed with an abundance of Yin the Synthesizer in your life. If Yang the Analyzer is in excess, however, you'll notice an army of thorny briars standing guard over your sense of self, threatening to choke the more tender blossomings of your mind and deny you a great deal of beauty that is otherwise yours to enjoy.

As you gaze over your own secret spaces, if you seem to feel some "knowledge of a lack," and experience from that a heart-stirring—a yin for change—be encouraged that there are some tried and true ways to have for yourself more "silver bells and cockleshells and pretty maids all in a row."

Obviously the creative arts—singing, dancing, painting and drawing, sculpting, making pottery, writing poems and stories or even keeping a journal, and so on—are fertile yin playgrounds, and proficiency in the arts indicates healthy access to Yin Mind. It's certainly a good idea, then, to improve or "find" your hidden artistic genius, with books and tapes and classes galore to help you. But there are other routes to Yinville. All that's really needed is to *want* to go. Motivated to change, you'll find ways to get there, guaranteed. For now, for starters, you might explore the scenic pathways plotted on the next few pages.

CLOUD GAZING

The cartoonist Gahan Wilson in *The New Yorker* magazine drew a man and child holding hands underneath cottony puffs of clouds. The little boy is pointing skyward. The caption reads, "That's a cloud, too. They're all clouds."

In his cartoons Gahan Wilson frequently points to the more frightening aspects of human behavior. Our bias toward "objective" phenomena is, to me, too, scary.

A cloud is cirrocumulus, not hippopotamus. But ask my two-year-old son. On a Gulf beach outing early this summer he pointed to the evening sky and said, "It's a crab, Dad!" And there low in the western bowl of coming night, backlit in orange, was a huge elongated cloud-crab with claws raised, a menace to all the population of Lower Alabama.

Consider the wisdom that issues forth from the mouths of babes and get yourself outside to gander at the clouds. Keep looking until the meteorological stuff clicks off and mare's tails and mackerel scales and fat angels and dog faces appear. They will paint themselves visible before your eyes because they *are there*. In the same way powerful insights lurk in the mists of your unconscious mind, waiting to synthesize for you knowledge on matters as globally "distant" as the stock market and poetry.

Go ahead, then—doctor's orders—enjoy a regular diet of Emerson's "daily bread" and watch your Yin Mind grow bigger and stronger with every bite.

MEDITATION

Remember how Betty Edwards was able to put to use what she believed to be the left brain's low threshold of tolerance for behavior it found illogical, irrational, or just a waste of time? How, if presented with a task it did not believe in, so to speak, the left brain would "sign off," leaving the right brain in charge, and there would emerge this almost unbelievable artistic ability?

You may use the same technique to bring Yin Mind to the head table. Engage in something "silly" like meditating and Yang Mind will rebel. It is not about to hang around for something as goofy as simply sitting, trying to empty your mind when its biggest kick is to cram it full of teeming data.

Bookshelves in libraries and bookstores are sagging nowadays under the weight of advice on how to meditate. And, basically, what they all offer us are ways to stop the rattle and hum, the yammer in our minds. It sometimes seems there is a stampede of voices all crying out to be heard and the best we can do is to cultivate a trail boss who can ride herd on the lot and keep us from going over the rocky precipice.

You can find meditational techniques that involve your whole body, like t'ai chi or yoga, which are good for those of us who cannot sit still. You may chase all the frenetic thoughts from your mind with the silent repetition of a mantra. You may try closing your eyes and simply listening with focus but without judgment to all the sounds that reach your ear. You can stare at your big toe or your navel. Look around at books and audio tapes and try one style of meditation and then another until you find one you will actually *do* and not just talk about to your friends at the coffeehouse.

What we're looking for in meditation is what Chopra called the "gap between our thoughts." If we can wiggle into such a gap, we find ourselves in a blissful silence on the other side of the wall of our thoughts. What's out there? Most metaphysical thinking agrees we'll find nothing less than an encounter with the Creator.

But if nothing else you are guaranteed a delicious *rest* from all the fracas and fray of your thoughts. Physicians are learning, too, that meditation can bring about powerful enhancements to the immune system when our minds stop creating so much stress, a product of perception. Most people go "zero at the bone" at the sight of a snake, but there are those rare few who want to take the slithery fellows home.

All the meditation techniques in one way or another involve the breath. In t'ai chi, rhythmic breathing accompanies the paired steps in the form—breathing in on the yin retreating motions and breathing out on the yang advancing motions.

In one very old and very powerful form of breathing meditation—done sitting, spine erect, with eyes closed, which produces instant alpha waves—you simply speak or sing "om" as the breath leaves the body. For reference and more detail on how to do this, check out Wayne Dyer's excellent audio tape *Meditations for Manifesting.* He declares that the sound "ah" is nothing less than the sound of the Creator and creation, that we find that sound in the name for First Cause in all religious traditions: God, Allah, Krishna, Buddha, Rah, Yahweh; and that "ah" is the utterance of procreation during orgasm.

When I listened to the tape I thought, too, of baby's first words: *mama, dada;* of *amen.* I tried to get *love* into the scheme, and couldn't decide if "uh" counts. Probably. I thought of Native Americans chanting "hey yah, yah, yah." I was disappointed that my favorite Teacher, Jesus, lacked the *ah* in the calling of his name—until I remembered Jesus is the Greek version of Yehoshua, what his Aramaic-speaking friends would have called him.

I thought of the well-known tale of editor Norman Cousins laughing his cancer into remission and figured "ha ha ha" carries the healing power of God. No time to meditate? Just "laugh your head off." Get rid of the thoughts in your head and let your lungs and diaphragm and belly run things for awhile and cure what ails you.

Studies have actually shown that moaning, too, is curative and enhances the healing process. So next time you're laid up in bed with the flu and feel like moaning, but tough-guy yang won't let you because, after all, John Wayne would be quiet and bite the bullet, send them both out of the room and do it anyway.

A most beautiful dialogue concerning the "sound of God" concept occurred between Joseph Campbell and Bill Moyers in *The Power of Myth— Masks of Eternity.*

Joseph Campbell: AUM is a word that represents to our ears the sound of the energy of the universe of which all things are manifestations. You start in the back of the mouth, *ah,* and then *oo,* you fill the mouth, and *mm* closes the mouth. When you pronounce this properly, all vowel sounds are in the pronunciation. AUM. Consonants are here regarded simply as interruptions of the essential vowel sound. All words are thus fragments of AUM, just as all images are fragments of the Form of forms. AUM is a symbol, a symbolic sound that puts you in touch with that resounding being that is the universe. And when you hear some of these Tibetan monks chanting, when they sing the AUM, you know what it means, all right. . . .

Ah, oo, mm—the birth, the coming into being, and the dissolution that cycles back. AUM is called the four element syllable . . . *ah, oo, mm* and the *silence* out of which it arises, and back into which it goes, and which underlies it.

Now, my life is the *ah, oo, mm*—but there is the silence that underlies it and that is what we would call the immortal. . . .

Bill Moyers: The meaning is essentially word-less.

Campbell: Yes. Words are always qualifications and limitations.

Moyers: And yet, Joe, all we puny human beings are left with is this miserable language, beautiful though it is, that falls short of trying to describe—

Campbell: That's right, and that's why it is a peak experience to break past all that, every now and then, and to realize *'Oh . . . ahh . . .'*

Words, if you remember, are the weapon of choice of Yang Mind. When your mind is full of words, the crowd is like a No Vacancy sign to Yin Mind. When room is made for yin thinking at the inn of your consciousness, it will come in on the single word AUM or OM—which *was* in the beginning, with God, and *is* God—leaving you not speechless, however, but in possession of the Source of all other words. And these other words

may produce *The Sound and the Fury* or the
Theory of Relativity or a marriage vow.

If your want further provocation about the
power of sound, of vibrating resonance, load into
your wheelbarrow Rupert Sheldrake's *Presence of
the Past—The Habits of Nature.* In a nutshell, he's
working from a theory that the "suchness" (a
good Zen word) of all things—trees, birds, rocks,
human bodies—emanates from a morphic resonance *outside* the thing being formed. But the
thing formed contributes changes to its own
recipe by changing its habits, thus amending all
future behavior and structure of all things like it.

The morphic recipe, so to speak, for humans
does not include the talent for sailboarding *until* a
bunch of cool California kids spend frazzling
months perfecting the ability. At some point, the
Universe agrees to include sailboarding skills in
the suchness of Being Human.

Now when the cool Florida kids give
sailboarding a try, they find it relatively easy to
learn since the techniques for mastery are now
there for the taking from the resonant field, the
Om of God, from which humans spring. Think
about the "impossible four-minute mile" from this
perspective. Once a single runner had broken this
barrier, it also fell for countless other runners.

Consider, too, the same phenomenon apply-
ing, first, to independent simultaneous break-
throughs in scientific research Our friend Kekule
announced in 1858 that carbon is tetravalent and

can link itself to form long chains; Archibald Scott Couper made the same announcement at the same time. Think further about the "behavior" of *inanimate* objects—like crystals learning to "become" for researchers, sometimes simultaneously in different laboratories, and always with greater ease following the growth of the first crystal.

Morphic resonance puts intelligence inside *and* outside the thinking organism, which explains how ten million tiny fish in a "school" all turn left at precisely the same instant. It also would explain paranormal events like ESP or clairvoyance—the "psychic" would merely be reading, one might say, from the "book of life" wherein all things are written, all recipes for suchness recorded. Sounds like Plato was thinking down this path when he wrote his Theory of Ideas, and believed that a thing cannot exist unless and until a *perfect* idea precedes it. And it's into this morphic resonance of perfect ideas that Yin Mind goes for those *Aha!* insights of creativity.

Perhaps more importantly, accessing the field of all possibilities through meditation will lead, in time (at least weeks of regular "practice"), to what a Zen Buddhist might call *mindfulness*. In mindfulness you have the service of a mighty steward of your consciousness, able even in our noisy pushy world to manifest a silent and grateful mind resonating with joy and peace. Like a cat sleeping, yawning, stretching while the raucous blue jay fusses and threatens her from a branch nearby.

MUSIC

Listen to music. But you listen to music already, you say, and Yang Mind is still firmly in control of your thinking? Maybe you aren't really *listening* to music. Eyes closed, with a real focus of your attention on the instruments separately and together—now the French horn, now the viola; first the lead guitar and next the synthesizer—really hear the music rise and fall on the rhythm of your breathing, the percussion of your heart. Imagine the look on the musician's face as she lifts her trumpet, as he chords his guitar. Tap out the beat with your foot. Let your awareness float on the melody. Listen to the words as they are sung.

Don't analyze anything. When you focus your awareness, Yang Mind wants to intellectualize and criticize the experience, take it apart, label and categorize then put it back together. Just listen wholly. Yang Mind will soon get bored and will leave you alone with the music to enjoy it all cuddled up with Yin Mind.

AFFIRMATION

Anthropologist Carlos Castenada learned that we don't know what we think we know and that there is actually a "separate reality" (the name of one of his books) that we may know if we will dedicate ourselves to learning of it. He became the pupil of a Yaqui Indian sorcerer, Don Juan, who told him, among other things, "If you stop telling yourself the world is so and so, the world will stop being so and so."

Now think about this before you start up with me about not brooking the advice of sorcerers, and that Castenada is either crazy or a liar or both: most of you will not call Jesus a crazy lying sorcerer when he said, effectively, the same thing: "If you tell the mountain to haul itself down to the sea, move over and watch it happen." Neither are many willing to disclaim his miracles. But are you listening to the part when he says that even the least among you can do what he did *and more!* Cognitive commitment the size of a mustard seed, he said, is all that's needed.

You get baby bites of comprehension of the power of your consciousness to bend "reality" when you participate in the placebo effect. I give you a sugar pill to combat the cancer in your lungs but tell you it is the most powerful anti-cancer drug ever developed. And because you are desperate and believe everything that doctors tell you, you accept the "medicine" expecting miraculous results.

You know what? Your body, responding to its master—your "cognitive commitment"—will sometimes (and we only need that one white crow) actually manufacture anti-cancer drugs of its own. And at the other end of the healing spectrum, remember what we told you earlier about how the patient of Dr. Swaim's willed her human life to end. Mark Twain made the cognitive commitment to live until the return of Halley's comet. He did, then lay down to die of natural causes.

Norman Vincent Peale (you *knew* his name would come up here, didn't you?) said if you want a quality, pretend you already have it. Goethe goes a step further outside the realm of self or ego and recommends: "Treat people as if they were what they ought to be and you help them to become what they are capable of being." For that matter, why not treat yourself as if you were *already* what you are capable of becoming, and help yourself become what you ought to be.

Our prophecies with children are remarkably self-fulfilling. Want a fat kid? Just keep telling her she's gonna be fat and so she will become. Instead, why not fill the child of whatever age—it's never too late to become what you might have been— with love and self-esteem and ability by telling them and *treating* them as if they were full of love and self-esteem and ability.

You can gorge yourself on the power of mind over matter by boning up on quantum physics. I'll entice you to at least learn a little about it by telling you that physicists have learned that the *quality of your attention* can *alter the outcome* of a legitimate laboratory experiment. Like, if you want light to be a waveform, it will be so. But if you want light to be a particle form, it will be that also. This is one of many "quantum mysteries" scientists are trying to unravel.

That all stuff is made of *non*stuff is another brain teaser. The "building blocks of nature," atoms, are made up of electrons, protons, neutrons, and things that are *not solid matter* at all. They are, instead, impulses of energy and intelligence that scientists may wind up calling super strings (no kidding). Only the *arrangement* of the little buggers accounts for the difference between chicken feathers and gold! Ask a physicist.

To me, one of the weirdest occurrences within quantum phenomena is something called "phase transition." Imagine you have been hired to realign a whole bunch of electrons—say a million of them. Sounds like a lot of work, but times are hard and you need the money. A quick lesson or two and it's off to work.

Here you go, one electron lined up the way the boss requested . . . two electrons lined up . . . three . . . and so on until at 199,000 you are totally sick of this and you are thinking, "One more of these suckers, then that's it. They can take this job and shove it!" Lo and behold, you twist that one last electron into place and *presto!* the other 800,000 line up *by themselves!*

"Hey, do I still get paid for the whole lot of 'em, boss?" Sure, why not? The physicists were expecting it. They call it "non-locality" and it mystifies them that one thing can physically effect another thing without making "physical" contact. Sorry, Sir Isaac. But it must have been good for the three hundred or so years it lasted.

The real You, the thinker behind your thoughts that says, "This is *my* elbow, this is *my* body, *I* was telling my*self* just the other day" is incredibly powerful and actually *can* move mountains down to the sea. All you need to do is clear the air of some of the static and improve the lines of communication with Yin Mind.

And one way is to simply say *no!* to the yammering of familial, social, cultural, prepackaged beliefs that have your consciousness behaving in a lopsided yang manner. You wouldn't tell a beautiful child that she is a dullard who is denied access to the farthest reaches of imagination. Well, don't tell yourself that either.

WALKS

Henry David Thoreau put great stock in walking as a way to stir him to thoughtfulness and creativity. He even claimed that the length of time he spent on his morning walk no less than determined the length of time he could expect to write well in the afternoon.

Yang Mind is the no-frills, busy one, serious and sober. Just saying "I'm going out for a walk"

freezes yang thoughts in their tracks. They don't
want to go for a walk. They want to study the
new tax laws, *something,* anything but get out into
the unprocessed air for a leisurely stroll.

And leisurely it should be if you want to get
all the yin you can from it. A set route, a deadline
for return, is way too yangy. Just follow your
nose toward the smell of a neighbor's baking
bread, your ear toward the golden retriever's
playful yelps or the seagull's bewitching cackle,
your eye in sight of the rising moon. Follow the
lead of the warm Southern breeze tickling the soft
hairs on your arm. Put on your Nikes—or bra-
zenly barefoot it—and just do it.

And if your want your walk to be like a sure-
enough meditation, you might try what some
people are calling "mindful walking." Repeat a
word or phrase in cadence with your steps and in
a short distance the silent chant will begin to
produce a trance-like effect.

Naps

I helped a friend of mine, a lawyer, move his
office furniture into a new office when he
relocated to the Gulf Coast, to Mobile, from
Tuscaloosa in the middle part of the state. After a
couple of desks and file cabinets, we came to a
bed—mattress, box springs, frame . . . even a box
marked "bed linens."

"Now wait a minute," said I, "what's the nature of the business you'll be conducting in this office?"

"Shame on you! Of course I will conduct the practice of law from this office. But I will also lay *myself* down here. Right after lunch for an hour or so most days of my working week. I will retire to this twin bed alone, for a nap."

"You've got to be kidding."

"Try, then, just try, to reach me during the aforementioned time frame. If my secretary is to keep her job, she will say to you and all others—well, except *judges*, of course—that I am in court. And there in that box of sheets is a small tasteful sign that plainly reads 'court.' That sign attaches here—" and he pointed to two small screw holes in the headboard. He then explained to me there had been a barber in his small, rural hometown who lived to be a hundred and four. "Harvey declared to all that it was his daily hour-long nap that kept him going 'past his time.' May the technique serve me so well." That was sixteen years ago and my friend still is in "court" far more than most of his colleagues.

Check the biographies of inventors and writers, artists and musicians and you might be surprised to find how often naps are mentioned in connection with the birth of some of their best ideas. Obviously, it's the yin-dominant dream state of mind that is yielding the goods for these people.

One difference, for many of us, between napping dreams and sleeping dreams will probably be a greater ease of remembering the content of the nap dreams. We don't cycle into the deeper levels of sleep where many of us would forget the dreams that had occurred in the earlier stages. When napping, we remain in the lighter REM (rapid eye movement) stage of sleep where dreams are so prolific.

I must remember to ask my friend how often his naps have helped him with just the angle he needs to win his client's case. There is incredible creativity available in a dreaming mind. A half-sleeping Yin Mind state was so important to Thomas Edison's creativity that he taught himself to doze in a chair while holding metal ball bearings above a pan. If he fell asleep he'd drop the bearings and awaken himself, then ease back into "the zone" that served him so well.

Lollygagging

Here is a true artform made flesh in a beautiful word, "lollygagging." In the dictionary it means to waste time, and there is a pejorative ring to the definition. You can just about see the Puritan Work Ethic getting itself all in a bother over the prospect of lollygagging.

But I would add to the definition that it is time "wasted" doing just what you *want* to do, for no good reason whatsoever. And before your little capitalist heart hammers its way right out of your chest, just remember that it is this slack time that so often yields that *Aha!* idea worth millions. Now I've got your attention.

So then what's a good lollygag thing to do? Well, Yang Mind despises the pointless behavior of, say, whittling, the art of carving a piece of wood all the way down to nothing. No sculpting. No rules. No usefulness. Makes no sense. Great! Guess who gets free roam of your brain? Scattering little diamonds of creativity all over the place.

So have fun with this one. Go out and waste some money on a pretty folding knife with excellent high-carbon steel blades. Get yourself a nice chunk of wood—it could have "soul" if well-chosen, say a sliver of board from your grandfather's barn . . . you get the picture. Sit in a comfortable, cool spot outside. (Don't dare think of sweeping the shavings.) And whittle. Perhaps while you whistle. Or be a bear of little brain and hum a little hum. Just whittle. You know what's ironic? Whittling helps *uncarve* the block for you.

Another friend of mine plays solitaire. Even if he is concentrating while playing, he has plenty of time for free-ranging thought during lazy, over-long shuffles of the deck.

This whole Yin Mind business is about creativity, remember, so think up a good lollygag for yourself, sit back and watch the spaces between your thoughts widen until there's room enough

108

for you to wiggle in for a break from all the clutter of worries and frets that bother your peace of mind.

SERVING

A nd the last among you shall be first—so the saying goes. That's how I view putting this suggestion at the end of our list. If drawing an upside-down vase gives Yang Mind the jitters, this notion will fairly rattle its cage for most men. *Learn to make gumbo and serve it to guests in your home.*

You may, of course, be from a backwater bayou in Louisiana and already know how to cook up the best gumbo in the parish. That's okay. Jump in ahead of the "learning" stage. For the rest, pick up three or four cookbooks and look at the seafood gumbo recipes. If there is not a gumbo recipe in the cookbook, toss it in the trash! From the recipes you have looked at, make up your own version, and experiment until it tastes good.

Now invite some friends over and cook in front of the them. Cut up the celery, peel the shrimp . . . everything, with your guests looking on. Do *everything* by yourself: set the table (and clean up afterwards), prepare the drinks. *Serve.* Your ego will not like it a bit, all this being "beneath your station." But Yin Mind, lord of humility and service to others, will revel in the preparation of a meal and serving it. Most women do this all the time, one of the proofs that they are kinder and gentler.

In a Zen Buddhist monastery, one of the six officers is called the *tenzo,* a place of highest honor. It is the tenzo's duty to feed the monks, including the gathering and washing of vegetables, menu decisions—the whole kitchen thing. Serving others in this most basic of ways is craggy yin for sure and a great way to massage your spirit.

HABITS

But your most bountiful harvest of Yin Mind will come from changing your habits. For many, being waited on is standard procedure and a habit in need of amendment. But all habits—though seemingly a comfort and source of security—short-circuit your ability to "choose again" and thereby modify outcomes for the better. Habits form what the Sufis call the *commanding self:* a mixture of primitive and conditioned responses, common to everyone, that inhibits and distorts human progress and understanding. And if habits are that much an inhibition to our transformation in consciousness, then the topic deserves its own chapter.

Seven

BUT THAT'S HOW I'VE ALWAYS DONE IT

If you think changing your habits means varying the order of your morning routine, it does, and more. It also means changing your habitual ideas. In fact, you could say that changing your *active* habits (eating soup holding the spoon in your off hand) is at a grade school, "penny" level, and changing your *contemplative* habits (voting your party when the other side clearly has a better idea) is at the PhD, "dollar" level. But a penny here, a penny there, first thing you know you'll have a dollar. Let's have a look.

Our active habits are the routine behaviors, often culturally imprinted, that we repeat so often they become automatic, requiring and *getting* almost no attention. "Under most ordinary circumstances, our lives are so predictably arranged that unconscious habits are adequate to get us where we want to go," is the way LaBerge put it in *Lucid Dreaming*.

Bernard McGrane, an undergraduate professor of sociology at Chapman University (Orange, California) challenges his students to answer an essential question: Where does society end and myself begin? McGrane's written a book called *The Un-TV and the 10 MPH Car* where he explores just how mindless most of us have become in the face of our habits.

Emerson declared that society is a joint-stock company and the commodity in greatest demand is conformity. McGrane makes assignments to his students that help them learn how strongly they conform and to what degree society controls them:

• Stand doing nothing in a busy place for ten minutes and observe the growing feeling of discomfort, a feeling of conspicuousness that arises when you are not allowed to "camouflage" idleness by either glancing at your watch or sitting down.

• Step onto an elevator and remain facing the rear—*all* passengers on the elevator get nervous with this one.

• Sit and watch an un-plugged TV for half an hour and note how the fear of lollygagging screams at you to get up and do something, *anything*, then be honest about how much of what you do (including work, hobbies, even spiritual practices) you stick into that "nothingness" just to take up space. Blaise Pascal said that all the problems of mankind stem from the fear we have of sitting alone in a room with nothing to do.

Pascal and McGrane would agree that we have cultivated our habits into a "habit of being." And with it has come the awful imbalance of yang, keeper of our habits. Robert (*Lila)* Pirsig's "metaphysics of quality"—divided, remember, into Dynamic Quality and static quality—calls static quality a "latching mechanism" whose best use is to hang onto the good stuff in our lives. Trouble is, of course, static yang, being also extremely aggressive, latches hard onto *everything*, trying to hold on *forever.*

Philosopher Lin Yutang (*The Importance of Living*) might say that yang is an obedient soldier and yin is a recalcitrant scamp. Yang will herd like cows and yin will scatter like monkeys. "Dictators and cows go well together, dictators and monkeys don't." Yutang comes down on the side of the scamp, saying that our "contrary-mindedness is the only hope for civilization." But it seems to me humanity is best served by cows who rebel, monkeys who herd. Yin and yang in balance. Picasso learned the rules, *then* broke them.

But most of us get stuck. We become slaves to our habits. Some guess that we have 50,000 or more thoughts a day—and 99 and 44/100 percent of them are exact replicas of the previous day's thoughts. However you feel about jazz and rock'n'roll today, you will probably feel tomorrow. Your Democrat and Republican persuasions are dyed-in-the-wool. Our contemplative habits are particularly pernicious. "A sect, party, or denomination is a device to save a body from the vexation of thinking," said Emerson.

What you're doing is forming a filter with your habits, through which you pour your life. And the way it puddles defies Chaos Theory—it looks the same day after day after day. Imagine your musical tastes as one thread in the filter, your political beliefs another thread, your racial attitudes another, your notions about money another, your fashion statement and religious affiliation and automobile preference—all these ideas actually become *you.* And you are the same yesterday and today and forever, one might say. This filter of your habits becomes a sticky web holding you in one place, where you wait to be devoured, sooner or later, by your foolish consistency.

But isn't God, as the Ordering Principle in the universe, habitual and consistent? Isn't that why we describe what we understand of natural phenomena as the *laws* of nature? And ought we not model ourselves in the image and likeness of God, Who is consistent?

No, because we don't know what God is like. Not even Moses was given a look at God. God knows what He is like and will do His own modeling. "Let go and let God," as my Twelve-Step friends suggest, and without effort we will be made into what God would have us made into.

One turn-of-the-century Russian philosopher by the name of George Ivanovitch Gurdjieff (*Meetings With Remarkable Men*) found two huge blocks to "higher consciousness": (1) expressing negative emotions, which, he said, if viewed rationally, have zero effect on external conditions—whining about the neighbor's unkempt lawn, for instance—but take an incredibly harsh internal toll; and, (2) falling prey to our habits.

Colin Wilson's *The Occult* mentions Gurdjieff's disdain for habitual behavior:

> What happens is simple. We fall into a habitual mode of life. . . . One's inner world becomes as habitual and predictable as one's outer life. . . . The problem is to start fertilizing consciousness with bursts of 'newness' so one can develop. . . .
>
> From birth until the age of twenty-one, we grow physically and in every other sense. Changes take place inside us without our volition. Then it stops. We are so used to the changes taking place 'automatically' that we find it difficult to stop expecting automatic growth to continue. It doesn't and most people slowly ossify. If growth is to continue, unusual efforts must be made so that something continues to 'change' every day.

With the caveat, "Don't try this at home!" I'll tell you that Mr. G. believed so strongly in the anaesthetic properties of habit and routine that he would sometimes have an assistant put an undisclosed amount of gasoline into his automobile, which had no fuel gauge, and he would drive off into the dead of night until he ran out of gas. He did not know whether his car would come to a halt on a train track, in a "bad" neighborhood, or across the street from a noisy bar.

But wherever he found himself he would explore his circumstances for all the unexpected events they could yield. G. also, late in life, took a blanket and pillow into his car and drove it out of town and into a tree at a good rate of speed, just to see what would happen. At a minimum, it was not automatic behavior!

Habits blind and deafen us. To the former, an elderhosteler who was a retired engineering professor told me he made the point with his students by telling them they were about to be given a quick test, which all should ace if they followed one special instruction: treat all "plus" signs as "times" signs, and all "minus" signs as "divide" signs. Eighty percent of his students failed the test. To the latter, ask someone to remember a phone number and area code that you will slowly recite to them once. Instead of two three-digit prefixes, put four numbers in the second grouping, then the last three. You will stumble most people with this one. Both examples demonstrate the power and incredible inertia of habit.

Walker Percy wrote an essay called "The Delta Factor" that went to the heart of some of the questions Robert Pirsig asked in *Lila*, so he included an excerpt of the essay in his book: "Why is a man apt to feel bad in a good environment, say suburban Short Hills, New Jersey, on an ordinary Wednesday afternoon? Why is the same man apt to feel good in a very bad environment, say in an old hotel Key Largo, in a hurricane?"

Then Pirsig gives his own answer: "With Quality divided into Dynamic and static components, a way of approaching them emerges. A home in suburban Short Hills, New Jersey, on an ordinary Wednesday afternoon is filled with static patterns. A hurricane in Key Largo promises a *Dynamic* relief from static patterns."

My two year-old son gets himself into a holiday mood at the mere mention of going to Aunt Marcie's, and I believe a variation of the same relief from static home patterns is at play here.

What all this has to say about the development of Yin Mind is that Yang Mind is the creature of habit. Merely changing your habits reduces yang's hold on your consciousness with a concomitant invitation to Yin Mind, "Come, let's play!"

With a will to do so and practice you could even shift the balance—you have all those years to make up for, remember—the other way to a dominance of Yin Mind. What a hoot! You might even become eccentric, defined by your unique-

ness, and join the ranks of William Blake, Albert
Einstein, Lewis Carroll, Emily Dickinson, and so
many famous, infamous, and unknown others
whose eccentricity shares traits like nonconfor-
mity, creativity, curiosity, idealism, intelligence,
and bad spelling according to neuropsychologist
David Weeks in his book *Eccentrics: A Study of
Sanity and Strangeness.* We know by now that Yin
Mind, the mother of eccentricity, cannot be
bothered with such trivialities as spelling and
grammar. Editor Yang takes care of that, while
Yin Mind begs to offer you more of what you felt
when you were a child. All that wonder and stuff.

The way to recapture what you lost, what you
are losing, and what you will fail to find if you
aren't careful is to develop Yin Mind until balance
occurs with Yang Mind. At a point of *perfect*
balance No Mind will exist, for a thing lacking a
defining opposite cannot be known. That's why
in Jewish religious tradition YWYH was used as a
name for the Creator: lacking vowels a word
cannot be spoken. The Tao says the Way that can
be spoken of is not the Way. So when we get our
yin and yang in perfect balance, the harmony that
results is that ineffable state of Nirvana, Heaven,
Enlightenment, Satori, Salvation . . . whatever
you want to call it.

How many can we find who are truly happy,
whose happiness doesn't come and go at the
mercy of circumstances, whose sense of well-being
is not fragile as a blown-glass figurine? Since the

answer is "not many," it is safe to say that full-tilt yang ain't working. Therefore, we might as well follow Jesus' suggestion to work on becoming perfect and get our yin and yang in sync.

For the hardware-oriented, brain researchers call this condition of balance "hemispheric synchronization." It is actually visible on an electroencephalograph, which measures brain waves. Left and right hemisphere brain wave patterns that are ordinarily quite different become virtually the same. The rare condition is marked by increased problem-solving ability and heightened awareness.

Without driving into a tree on the outskirts of town, what can we do to shake loose from our habits, live freely and meaningfully in our society instead of our society living us? I don't need to answer that. You know—we all know. Krishnamurti (*The Awakening of Intelligence*) said that our questions are a clever device for holding at bay answers we have always had but which we do not want to hear.

Penny changes in our habits are probably the most effective, least threatening way. Not only is change scary to you, it's scary to those around you. If you have decided to embark upon this mission of developing Yin Mind for better balance in your thinking, you might want to share your intentions with some of those closest to you. And *don't* let this become a yang-directed announcement. Yang Mind wants to take over all your plans, even one to reduce its influence in your thinking, and handle it like a battle plan. Let yin's "kinder, gentler" way lead you through telling others of your desire to become more creative and spontaneous, more like the child Jesus suggested you must become in order to find Heaven *inside of you.*

A few pennies-from-Heaven ideas will lead to dollars' worth of differences in the feeling you get just looking at the sky, your patience in the checkout line at the grocery store, and the way you do all the things you do. How you cook a pot of gumbo, change a flat tire. Shaking habits is all you need to get you started down the path toward the joy of more Yin Mind. For instance, take a look at these habit-busting tips:

• Order your dessert first next time you eat out. Yang Mind is already screaming. "You can't do that. It will ruin your appetite!" Okay, but maybe your appetite could use a little spoiling. If not, you'll be surprised how easy it is to do baked salmon after key lime pie.

• Park in the *first* parking spot you come to in the shopping center parking lot, way out there on the edge where no other person parks. You won't get dings in your door, for one thing. Best of all, Yang Mind will refuse to see the sense in your "illogical" behavior and you'll make the stroll with Yin Mind humming a little hum in your ear.

• How do you take your coffee? For forty-three years, black with a little sugar. So have a cup with cream and sugar, try a cup black with no sugar. Decide in advance to suspend the "yuck" while trying to see what it is your wife, for instance, finds to enjoy in her coffee.

• You've never had on shorts and sandals "in public"? Go for it. Put on a little smile first and you will be looking "mahvelous, dahling, simply mahvelous."

• Which hand do you brush your teeth with? Next time use the other one. For you hardware types, it goes something like this, ultra-simplified for the sake of keeping to the thin-book promise: Imagine a circle that represents your brain. Draw an X somewhere on the circle—that's the impulse to act, to brush your teeth. Now draw another X somewhere else—that's the activity, the motor skill of brushing your teeth. Draw a line between the two—that's the neural pathway from desire to action. It's been taking the same route for half a century. It is a mighty deep rut.

Switch hands and you get the same result: clean teeth, or close, at least. Maybe some foamy spatters on your shirt. The real payoff, though, is that you sparkled some different synapses by going down a different road. From this you could get a chain reaction leading to a new insight or intuition, say, about which new stock to invest in. So for brushing your teeth with your other hand you become an overnight multimillionaire featured on an episode of "Lifestyles of the Rich and Famous." Pretty cool, huh?

You get the point and can make a list of harmless static-pattern interrupts a mile long. But go the extra mile and dabble with your contemplative habits, too. If you are a life-long Democrat and the Republican on the other end of the block comes up with a better way to school our kids, for Heaven's sake side with *thinking* and vote for the better idea.

"If you always do what you do, you always get what you get," is the advice of Michael Murphy, who leads golf workshops around the country and has a book to sell, *Golf in the Kingdom.* Michael will have you tee off into the rough, intentionally but without telling anyone else your intentions. He'll have you notice how your elbow and neck resist letting you do such a foolish thing. That's right, Yang Mind is pulling those strings to make your neck tighten. It cannot abide such a bizarre waste of time.

But it's not a waste. If you go ahead and make the shot into the rough, you've essentially told your yang caddy to take a little time off. Yin makes the shot, loving the playfulness. The short of the long? The techniques Murphy teaches *work.* Strokes come off your game.

Do something different and get different results. Einstein said we ought not to expect solutions from the mindset that created the problem. If we keep fighting with our wives over the same thing, keep yelling at our kids about the same thing, the fight will always have the same yucky ending. If you always do what you do, you will always get what you get; give it up and say *maybe* I am looking at this all wrong. That subtle switch, like whacking the ball into the jungle, will be enough to invite a different outcome.

So keep up the good work, and on the ride home from the course, turn to some jazz music if you don't like jazz, classical if you hate long-haired music . . . and *listen*. Unclench your jaw and really try to discover why others delight in this music that you detest. Better yet, listen to a style of music you don't like with someone who does. Hitchhike on their pleasure. Sit down with your teenager and pat your foot while she bobbles her head and croaks weird lyrics. Watch what happens to how you feel inside after two or three suspicious sidelong glances in your direction are metamorphosed into a grin.

And if you really want to shake, rattle, and roll your Yang Mind, have a go at one of your extreme prejudices. If there is a race you hate, a skin color that makes you paranoid, a religion that riles you, then set about to shine a light of understanding into the dark corner of your ignorance, for that's all it really is.

Begin with books (that wheelbarrow is getting a workout) that offer you history, biographies, art. Try to imagine what it must be like to be one of *them*. Then, when you feel safe to try, meet and talk with someone whose religion or color has frightened you. "Do [or know] that which you fear and watch fear disappear," said Winston Churchill. Push the paradigm of your understanding until a new paradigm emerges—allowing that this paradigm, too, is replaceable when something more sensible and useful is discovered.

In our yang-driven urge to cover all the contingencies, to have a plan for everything that could *possibly* come down the pike, it would be well to hear again that men make plans and God smiles. Life *refuses* to be habitual—so you might as well learn to let it be more organic and resist habitual actions and thought patterns.

You only *think* the way you do it is the best way to do it. Do you *really* know when anything is in your best interest? Did you catch one of the two or three TV news magazine pieces on what became of the lives and happiness of million-dollar lottery winners. I mean, we *all* believe it would be in our best interest to win the lottery, right? All the winners interviewed said things were great for a while—before turning real sour. One guy's brother shot off half his face for cutting off the flow of loans. Another woman lost her husband *and* custody of her kids. I'm drawing up an outline for a book called *Lessons of the Lottery— How to avoid wrecking your life when you become an instant millionaire.*

Yin Mind understands what the prophet Mohammed meant when he said, "My poverty is my pride." Yin Mind understands, too, why Jesus didn't ask Joseph of Arimathea to give up *his* riches. It was not capricious favoritism. Jesus knew Joseph wasn't hooked on his loot.

Dag Hammarskjold, former Secretary General of the United Nations, is included as a modern-day mystic in a book by Georgia Harkness, *Mysticism—Its Meaning and Message*. She calls to the reader's attention Hammarskjold's posthumously published journal *Markings* and this entry: "I don't know Who—or what—put the question, I don't know when it was put. I don't even remember answering. But at some moment I did answer *Yes* to Someone—or Something—and from that hour I was certain that existence is meaningful and that, therefore, my life, in self-surrender, had a goal. From that moment I have known what it means 'not to look back,' and 'to take no thought for the morrow.'"

Don't be afraid to surrender to uncertainty. Even financial uncertainty. We all arrive at the same port anyway, so lighten up, say yes, and better enjoy the ride.

Summary

AND NOW THE ALTER CALL

No matter what you have been led to believe, the world doesn't need fixing. It ain't broke. What the quantum physicists know of subatomic phenomena was happening before they knew it and will continue to happen if people blow themselves off this planet. Radio isotope studies show a total exchange of every atom and molecule in the human body in a little more than a year. The Ordering Principle in the universe staging this event does not require permission, advice, or complicity from DNA, the body, or the brain.

Nature doesn't need us to save her. If human behavior continues to devolve to a worst-case scenario, leaving a scorched and silent, barren-faced, ash-darkened Earth, be assured that Nature

will work her alchemy: in a thousand years or a
million years some dead seed will crack open,
unbend a root downward, and push a green and
growing face upward to praise the sun, which will
not have blinked at our foolishness.

All we need to do is what we came here to do
when we enrolled in this Earthly curriculum: to
lose our fear and learn to love perfectly.

The hellfire-and-brimstone preachers of my
youth during each church service would issue an
altar call, which always came as a relief to me
because it signaled the end of the sermon.
"Change your ways or go to hell," was the bottom line of the altar call.

This sermon being just about ended, it is time
for a last call to alter our minds, to develop a yin
for change and allow that field of all possibilities
to deliver us a better world. Change your mind
and watch the world change right before your
eyes into a place worth loving, peopled by people
who deserve our unconditional best regard.

Bodies, although they can link sexually,
cannot join to become one. Minds *can* become
one when joined in an idea like love. Philosopher
Mortimer Adler writes about the *Six Great Ideas,*
or the 102 Great Ideas discussed in his two-volume
Syntopicon. Love, of course, is one of the Great
Ideas. In this book Love goes at the top of the list.
All other ideas follow, and may be tossed up as
subject to philosophers' perennial debate. We
only need to see that our best thinking has not

corrected our relationships with others and to desire deeply that we change our thinking. What good is it to concoct a new scientific theory, write a great novel, cook the world's best pot of gumbo—or any other endeavor you wish to list— if it does not end the danger of your murder at a hamburger joint.

The *Course in Miracles* says that a "universal theology is impossible—a universal *experience,* on the other hand, is not only possible but necessary."

The reason we require a universal experience of love and forgiveness is self-evident. Its lack threatens to destroy us. But we haven't valued that experience above all things or it would be so. When president John Kennedy got this country stirred up to get a man on the moon, there was no question it would happen. We must join together and become motivated to change, to choose differently, *now,* and it does not take a rocket scientist to see why.

That we *can* love one another to even radical extremes is evident when we abandon the first law of nature, namely, self-preservation. Arthur Schopenhauer in the *Foundation of Morality* asks: "How is it that a human being can become so involved in the peril and pain of another that, without thought, he sacrifices his own *life* to the other? [It is the] breakthrough of a metaphysical realization that you and the other *are* one. And that the separateness we perceive and believe in are only an effect of the temporal forms of sensibility and our true reality is in our unity with all life. This is a difficult truth . . . ."

Difficult but necessary. The only reason to develop Yin Mind is that Yang Mind in dominance will not allow change. Every mind that seeks and accomplishes a balance of yin and yang, however, brings us a step closer to transformation. Like water dripping into a glass until it reaches the top and actually bulges beyond the top until, with one more drop, it overflows.

What is most exciting is that *you* can be the one to make the difference. But you don't need to fix the world. Simply balance yin and yang in your mind, which for most means a lot more Yin Mind. You just might win Heaven's Phase Transition Award for having the mind that changed and—click, click, click—all the rest of the dominoes fall. Then the human experience/experiment will have been a whopping success, just in the nick of time, giving back to God what he had all along hoped for from us: that we love one another. ❂